FOLLOW ME

The ABC's of Christianity

Shawn Spohn

authorHOUSE®

AuthorHouse™
1663 Liberty Drive
Bloomington, IN 47403
www.authorhouse.com
Phone: 1 (800) 839-8640

Unless otherwise noted, Scripture quotations are from the King James Version of the Bible.

KJVER, Word of God, Sword Study Bible, the Sword Emblem, Word for Word, and Red Letter Old are registered trademarks of Whitaker House.

Published by AuthorHouse 07/15/2019

ISBN: 978-1-7283-1622-2 (sc)
ISBN: 978-1-7283-1934-6 (e)

Print information available on the last page.

This book is printed on acid-free paper.

PREFACE

The Bible simply tells us to get rid of all sin in our life. James tells us that if we resist the devil then he will flee. The Bible tells us to draw near to God and He will draw near to us. We must follow the Lords Spirit and continue in His leadership and guidance to grow and become more like Christ. 1 Thessalonians 5:19 Quench not the Spirit. This will absolutely make lives peaceful and complete. There is an eternity and there are only one of two places to spend it, Heaven or Hell. We have written this book fervently praying to the Lord that people will come to know Him as their Lord and Savior. This book was written simple and is just the ABC's of Christianity. Our most devout prayer is that we may be used by the Lord to help glorify His kingdom. We kindly accept any compliments, questions, or conversations concerning this book, the Bible or anything concerning God. Thank you and God bless,

Shawn & Shannon Spohn

Contents

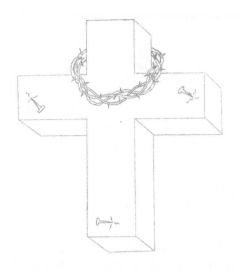

CHAPTER 1

God's Love

John 3:16 *For God so loved the world, that He gave His only begotten Son, that whosoever believeth in Him should not perish, but have everlasting life. * This verse is so strong and powerful. It is probably the best-known verse whether it is a sinner or saint that reads or hears it. To me this verse has so much meaning. When I gave my life to the Lord and He called to me then I was a sinful man. More wretched and sinful than anyone I knew.

When the Lord called me while I was yet a sinner, He died for me. (Romans 5:8). When we accept Jesus as our Lord and Savior then the Holy Spirit comes unto us and dwells within us, then we are stamped to be a child of God forevermore. To spend eternity with Him as we are sealed by His Spirit.

(Ephesians 1:13). When the Spirit comes upon us, He will show us all truth and righteousness. He will lead and guide our path as we walk on this earth. This is such a wonderful blessing and so much love is shown to us that God would send His holy Spirit to dwell within us that we may live uprightly and be led and guided by His Spirit. When I accepted Jesus Christ as my Lord and Savior, then I felt all the shame and all the dirty filthiness that my life had been thus far.

I cried and cried unto the Lord asking forgiveness for every single sin

1

that I could think of, that I ever committed in my life that was stored in my memory. I just went back as far as I could remember and ask forgiveness for every sin. This event lasted for days as every time I thought of a sin, then I repented of it with a true heart and it just tore me up. It brought me to tears in disgrace and shame for what I had done. When the Spirit comes upon us, we know right and wrong even in this sinful flesh.

Out of shame I felt wrong for all I had done. Our loving heavenly Father sent His only begotten Son to be tortured, beaten, afflicted, and ultimately crucified for our sins. A just man that never sinned while walking in this flesh and blood to show us the way to His righteousness. He never knew sin, yet He took on the sins of the whole world. (1 John 2:2). As Jesus walked this earth in the flesh and blood and was a sinless man, then He went to the cross suffered and died for us. This shows the amount of love that the Lord has for us. As we are here today and our Lord is long-suffering and loves us just as much as anybody could be loved, then we must look to the cross of Calvary to see what Jesus accomplished for us there.

This is truly never-ending love. This is an over- abundant amount of love that is perfected through Christ Jesus toward us. The Bible tells us that there is no greater love than that of a man lay down his life for his friends. (John 15:13). Once again, as while we were sinners then Jesus died for us. (Romans 5:8). The Lord loves us so much as His children that He sent His holy Spirit that dwells within every believer that we may live accordingly and as uprightly that we can in this sinful body.

We love God because He loved us first. (1 John 4:19). The closest we can come to understanding what love really is, would be the love a parent has for their child. We can try to raise our children the best we can but, ultimately, they make all their decisions as they grow older. Even when they make the wrong decisions, the bad decisions, then we still love them and try to help them accordingly. A parent's love for their children is probably the closest to unconditional love that we as humans in the sinful flesh and blood with our sinful nature can come to understand.

We can say I love you but, God's word tells us that actions speak louder than words. So, when we act accordingly and when we get the Lord involved in our lives, His love will shine through us and we become better people. Words are only words and actions show our true feelings and emotions. The closer we draw to God, the more His love is shed abroad within us. The closer we draw to God, the more His light shines through us. (Matthew 5:16). As we walk close to the Spirit of God then we act more Christ-like than before we were saved.

The Bible tells us that we shall be known by our fruits. (Matthew 7:16-20). This simply means that we, being Christians, should love. We should love the Lord, love our neighbors, love our enemies, and just simply love everyone because God is love. God tells me in His word, **(2 Timothy 1:7); *For God has not given us spirit of fear; but of power, and of love, and of a sound mind.*** With God's Spirit dwelling within us and if we are listening to the Spirit, then we should be led accordingly to walk the way that we should on this earth. Being led by the Spirit will give us the mannerism that we should act upon in all situations and toward all people that we meet. God is love. (1 John 4:7-8).

Our walk in this sinful nature is a conditional love. We have conditions on which we base our love. We are in this fallen state and we can say that we love one another but this is usually followed by a condition. We have heard it said before that people have fallen out of love or grown apart. If a drastic situation or circumstance arises in a relationship, then this could create a vengeful mix of emotions between the couple. If something bad happens to the other person concerning the relationship, then this will be dragged into a confrontational argument due to emotions. If a spouse were to cheat on another, being one of the worst situations possible, then the spouse that has been cheated on will have a very strong dislike or hatred toward their spouse. This is our human nature and I have been on both sides of this situation. This is where our conditional love comes in effect.

As we sin constantly under the Lord, His forgiveness is overwhelming and His faithfulness and justification through the blood of Jesus is what unconditional love becomes. It is an emotion and our emotions are inconsistent as opposed to God's. He is always and will forever be the same. As He was in the beginning, as He is now, as He will always be for all eternity. (Hebrews 13:8). God's love is unconditional and never changing. Before God sent His Son into the world to be crucified, and the blood of Jesus was shed for the atonement of our sins, then man had no chance.

Jesus gave us two great Commandments. The first great commandment to love the Lord with all our heart and with all our soul and with all our mind hangs our salvation points given to us by God's grace through His only begotten son Jesus Christ our Lord and Savior. There is nothing that we can do to gain this salvation because He gave it to us and through the knowledge of what the Lord has done for us by His grace we are saved. The Lord has given us this freely, so we need to be thankful for everything we have, who we are, and love the Lord thy God above anything and everything in this world. When the Holy Spirit calls a lost soul and they receive Jesus as their Lord and Savior, they shall be saved. (Ephesians 2:8).

This will get you to heaven for all eternity with our heavenly Father. In order to finish up the Christian walk we must understand the second great commandment; love thy neighbor as thyself. It's nothing that we can do, the Lord's Spirit that dwells within every believer must show us the way. This is not a love as you would love your mother, daughter, or your family but it is a different kind of love. It is a love that you don't take negative actions towards someone, not even your enemy, not someone who spitefully uses you, persecutes you, or does you wrong. You pray for these people because, we wrestle not in the flesh and blood but against the evil principalities and spirits of this world. (Ephesians 6:12).

When we love our neighbor and we get this second great commandment down deep in our heart then it embeds into our souls and in our minds. After this our spirit handles everything concerning our neighbors. We do love our neighbors and after we get this our Christian walk is more complete. This brings about peace, joy, and happiness with our spirit intermingling with the Spirit of God that dwells in us. God is love. (1John 4:16). He would rather us be as Christ-like as we can and that includes everything we do unto the Lord and so we must love one another as He loved us. (Colossians 3:23). satan uses people in our lives, he is smart, deceitful and attractive.

The only way that we as Christians have any chance to fight him off is by the strength of the holy Spirit, in which we rebuke him in Jesus powerful name. We only serve one Lord that is my Lord Jesus Christ, you cannot serve both God and mammon. (Matthew 6:24). You cannot be luke-warm, you must be hot or cold. (Revelation 3:15). I pray that you are hot for the Lord and are not teetering on the fence but, rather jump over onto the Lord's side, for it is the winning side. If you choose the losing side, you will be in hell's fire for all eternity with the devil and his angels.

4

There will be a massive amount of lost souls that have denied Jesus as their Lord and Savior. It would not be God's will that any of His children be lost and perish into hell's flame because, He created it for the devil and his angels. (Matthew 25:41).

I believe even a large percentage of Christians today that truly know Jesus as their Lord and Savior are not grasping on to our second great commandment. If you don't grasp onto the second great commandment and exercise the almighty Spirit of God that dwells within you then you are falling short of what you can do to help glorify the kingdom of God. You are not exactly in the center of His will. God desires to lead and guide us through His Spirit. We must listen and quench not the Spirit. (1Thessalonians 5:19).

Seek after the Spirit with everything that we have, seek ye first the kingdom of Heaven and all the rest shall follow. (Matthew 6:33). I desire only to plant, seed, and water. Just not a long time ago, I understand that the second great commandment, is one that brings about total joy and peace. For the Lord tells us to take His yoke for it is the easy way. (Matthew 11:30). That is true, its release's a big pressure and stress from our minds and makes life so much easier.

After I come to realize that loving my neighbor and praying for those that spitefully use me and realized that the Lord says vengeance is mine, now I let the Lord deal with my enemies and with those that do me wrong. (Romans 12:19). How much more peace and joy this has brought to my life. I can honestly, truthfully, and whole heartedly pray for people that have done me wrong and know that the Lord will take care of them accordingly. He will chastise them if they are Christians and have truly given their lives unto Him because, the Lord chastens those who He loves. (Hebrews 12:6).

Later in a testimony of this book, I will speak of the chastening hand of the Lord. I am so grateful that He has corrected me during my bad choices and decisions. The chastening that I underwent seemed difficult at the time but, as I look back, this has brought me closer to God than I ever have been. Through the chastisement of the Lord, I do truly have everything that I need, want, and desire. I completely understand the following two verses. (Job 5:17,

Deuteronomy 8:5-6). If they are not saved and have not given their lives over to our Lord and Savior Jesus Christ, then they will be punished and suffer eternal hellfire with the devil and his angels.

So, again it comes down to us overcoming the natural mind, the carnal mind that wants to wrestle with the flesh and blood. It is not against God's children, who we are to look at as our opposition, as they are just being led by satan and his dark forces. So, back to the first great commandment, love the Lord thy God with all your heart, all your mind, and all your soul. When we get this commandment in our hearts and are drawn as the Lord draws us to Himself through His Spirit then this is the time when we receive salvation through God's grace by the gift of His only begotten son Jesus Christ. When we believe that He was crucified on the cross by His blood we have been forgiven our sins.

It is by one man's sin, which was Adam, in the Garden of Eden, that we all have a sinful nature. It is by one man's work, Jesus the only begotten son of God, that we all who accept Him are forgiven our sins. (Romans 5:19). Thank you, Jesus. When we seek Him, His forgiveness and believe in our hearts that He died for us, then we are saved and the Lord has sent to us a comforter, a mediator with the Lord God called the holy Spirit. (John 14:16). When we start the day looking at all the blessings from the time, we open our eyes in the morning until the time we fall asleep at night and count them, then this will be pleasing unto the Lord thy God.

The Bible tells us to give thanks for everything we have. (Ephesians 5:20). The more thankful we are for the Lords love that He bestows upon us through His blessings every day, then the closer His Spirits draws unto us. I no longer believe in good karma and bad karma; I believe in blessings and chastisement of the Lord. I no longer believe in coincidence as I follow the Lord. I take the good with the bad and full heartedly believe that the Lord helps me along my way. Everything, I absolutely know, happens to me is for my best. The Bible tells me all things happen for the good of those that love the Lord. (Romans 8:28). Love the Lord with all your heart, with all your soul, and with all your mind. God is love...

God's love has built me a mansion in heaven, heaven is a place that the Lord has prepared for us when Jesus said He's going to prepare a place for us. (John 14:2-4). Heaven is for all Christians, all God's children, all that believe Jesus is their Lord and Savior. Heaven is a place for all eternity after our natural bodies return to the ground from whence, they came.

(Ecclesiastes 12:7). Heaven is where God wants all His children to be with Him one day. The Lord wants a personal relationship with each one of us. Therefore, he has given us freewill and we have choices in everything that we do. When we choose to accept Jesus as our Lord and Savior, then we have God's holy Spirit dwelling within us to lead and guide our paths until the day that He returns to gather His church. Forever more we will be with the Lord.

CHAPTER 2

1ˢᵗ Testimony

From the beginning, the Lord is on a mission, knowing all things; He is omniscient; all-knowing, all- wise, and all-seeing. The Bible says that He knows our souls and every hair on our head before we are born. (Galatians 1:15). The Lord knew that we we're going to choose Him, that we were going to accept Jesus as our Lord and Savior. Because of Jesus being crucified and through His blood being shed for the atonement of our sins, we now have an advocate with the Father. (1 John 2:1-2). Before we are even born the Lord knows if we are going to choose and accept Him. By God's grace we are saved through faith in Jesus. It is nothing that we can do but, it is simply a gift from God. (Ephesians 2:8).

So, we are pre-destined to be His children because the Lord chooses who He wants to be Christians, as He knows we have already chosen Him. (Ephesians 1:4). Just as He chose us before the foundation of the world, that we should be holy and without blame before Him. He works through Christians as well as lost people. Judas was one of the twelve apostles that was with Him every day and He knew that Judas was going to deny Him and so He used Judas as an important part of His plan to get these instructions (the love letter from the Lord, The Bible) to us so that we can study it and be approved unto the Lord. (2Timothy 2:15) He used this to carry out His plan to give us the living word that we now use as a guide to eternal peace and happiness.

I grew up in a big, loving family, a very close family but was never taken to church, I was kind of shy and quiet. I have a shy, quiet soul. I was 12 years old and satan just had me running wide open. I was stealing stuff, I was drinking, and just acting crazy. It just got worse and worse as I grew older. I was stealing motorcycles and vehicles when I was 14 years old and just didn't care about people.

As I got older and in high school, satan had me blinded and misled and I had such a big ego about everything I did. There wasn't anybody better, nobody had better stuff than I did, nobody could do anything better than me. So, I had this huge ego that got worse in college.

This is the opposite of what God wants us to have. We should always humble ourselves unto the Lord. (James 4:10). He wants us to love and help one another. (John 13:34). Treat everyone with kindness. I thought I was doing everything on my own and that I always had the right answers but that was the farthest thing from the truth. Little did I know, the Lord was there with me all the way through even though I was not doing the right thing. (Romans 5:8). Thank God our Lord is long suffering and very patient.

I married my high-school sweetheart straight out of college and over time we ended up having three children. I was a bad alcoholic, a womanizer, and just riotous all around. There was no good in me at all. Ultimately, she ended up divorcing me and about one year later come back and wanted to reunite and it was just impossible at that point in time. Neither one of us had the Lord in our lives and as I look back at it, how sad it was and what a terrible father and husband I was.

As a Christian father it is our responsibility to show our children the right path. (Ephesians 6:4). I failed miserably at doing this because she would not let me see the children or have a part in their lives. satan really helped me do a number at this point in my life. Just prior to our divorce, I had fallen asleep driving and was in a horrible car accident. There is no doubt I should have been dead instantly in this accident. I did end up with a very bad head injury out of the deal.

Ultimately, this has been most beneficial to me serving the Lord. God is always with us and always calling to us. We just need to turn toward Him and accept Jesus as our Lord and Savior. As I look back, through all

9

my nastiness the Lord was still there with me. There is absolutely no way I should have survived the accident and yet here I am. The Lord had a plan for me. (Jeremiah 29:11). Even after my near- death experience I still did not think nothing about the Lord. I was one of them people that just didn't believe in God, believe in satan, believe in evolution, believe in anything, but living for the moment. After I healed, I bounced back from that horrible accident and just started living more wretched than ever before.

I ended up finding myself in jail and felt like I had nobody and nothing. I was in a church service in jail and the Lord called to me and grabbed ahold of me. I did quench the Spirit at this time and didn't step up and profess Jesus as my Savior. The next week He called to me again and I confessed Jesus as my Lord and Savior and became inflamed for His word and to serve Him. All I did was read and study the Bible the remaining time I was in jail. It felt so good and I felt so free even though I was incarcerated. (John 8:36).

When we accept Jesus as our Lord and Savior then we are sealed by the holy Spirit. From this point on we have eternal salvation through the grace of God by faith in Jesus Christ our Savior. We will spend all eternity in heaven with our Lord, where He has gone to prepare a place for us. One day He will return to gather all His children. (John14:3). We are sealed with the holy Spirit. (Ephesians 1:13-14). After the Spirit seals us, which is the baptism of fire by the Holy Ghost, He dwells within us. Our bodies become a temple for the Holy Ghost, Gods Spirit dwells within every believer. (1 Corinthians 3:16). The Spirit was sent by Jesus to help comfort, lead, and guide us.

As we live in this flesh and blood then God's holy Spirit leads, guides, and gives us the strength we need to fight against the wiles of satan. (Ephesians 6:11). We must look to the Spirit for all answers, for all knowledge, and for all our strength. (2 Timothy 1:7). For we cannot do this walk alone because we are born into sin with this natural body and we need the Spirit to show us and guide us in all truth as we walk on this earth awaiting the return of Jesus. (Luke 3:16). (John 1:27). After we have received the Spirit unto ourselves and the Lord has drawn us unto Himself, then we must pursue the center of God's will for our lives. We must pray and meditate on what the Lord would have us to do. Always looking for His leadership and guidance. (1 Thessalonians 5:17).

The closer we are to the center of God's will for our lives, then the more peace, love, and joy we will experience as we walk in this flesh and blood. The closer to the center of God's will we are for our lives, then the more accordingly our prayers will be answered. We will pray for what the Father would have us to want and pray for what is best for us on this earth while we are waiting for the return of Jesus. So therefore, when we do find the center of His will for our lives, we will notice that our prayers are being answered more accordingly to the manor at which we are praying. We will pray for what the Father wants us to have in this life and it will be what we want in this life because we are walking uprightly. (Psalms 143:10).

As we continue to grow in our Christianity and become more Christ like, then we grow spiritually and become closer toward what God would have us to be. We will learn to love others. We will feel and learn the love of God. We will treat others as we would want to be treated and our souls will humbly seek the wisdom and guidance of Gods holy Spirit.

All Christians must confess with their mouth and believe with their hearts that Jesus is Lord and Savior. (Romans 10:9). Now, knowing this as we continue to grow, then the Bible tells us that we should go through water baptism. This is not part of the salvation plan but, it is important that we express ourselves publicly and confess that Jesus is our Lord and Savior through water baptism. Through water baptism we show that we are dead and buried with Christ, the old man is dead. We emerge out of the water to a fresh new life. Overall, water baptism shows that we are new creatures in Christ through the death and burial of the old man and the resurrection of the new man. This is a public confession. Jesus publicly called all His apostles.

We must fully live and try to follow the Spirit for His leadership and guidance for our lives. **(Romans 6: 4). *Therefore we are buried with Him by baptism into death: that like as Christ was raised up from the dead by the glory of the Father, even so we also should walk in newness of life.*** Our spirit was quickened and made alive as soon as we accepted Jesus into our lives after the holy Spirit called unto us. As Christians, satan will be trying to pull us away from the will of God. As we are drawn into the center of God's will, we will most assuredly help other Christians or help lost people. Therefore, it's very important to do and follow what the Spirit would lead and have us to do. The Lord will use us if we are willing and so desire and all Christians should desire to be used by the Lord to help glorify His kingdom. We should spread the gospel, the good news, so that others can hear and see what the Lord has done for us. We should let the light of Christ shine through us so that others may see. (Matthew 5:16).

As we are walking this walk, they should know us by our actions. (Matthew 7:16-20). satan will always try to attack us. Once we are sealed by the holy Spirit then our salvation is reassured for all eternity. satan will continually attack us to try and get us out of the center of God's will. If we walk the way the Lord would have us, then we will be planting and watering seed along our path that we may help lost people. satan knows all our weaknesses and how to try to get us out of the center of God's will. He will try to drag us down and try to use our weaknesses to pull us away from the Lord. satan is all desirable to the world and to someone who isn't strong in the Lord.

In my early Christian walk I was not strong in the Lord; my seed did not grow deep when the Lord first called me. This caused me to turn from the Lord's will as satan deceived me and put me in a less desirable place for a Christian to be. (2 Peter 2:22). (Proverbs 26:11). satan is so happy when a backslider has fallen off the path of God's will. This will enable satan to deceive the backslider more easily and pull them away from the glorification of the kingdom of God. As a backslider walks the wrong path, he is not letting his fruits be shown unto the lost. (Matthew 7:16).

You will not be efficiently used of the Lord when you don't give your whole spirit to Him. We cannot serve two lords. (Matthew 6:24). The Lord would not want someone lukewarm, either you are hot for the Lord or you are cold for the Lord. Lukewarm is not good in any way, shape, or form. (Revelation 3:16). So, as the back slider continues his sinful ways the Lord will still try to convict him through the Spirit that he needs to get back on the right path. (Proverbs 14:14).

The earlier in life a man gives his life unto the Lord and serves the Lord in the way we all should, then that person has a better state of mind and well-being. The backslider has broken free from his demons through the strength of the Spirit of God who quickens us. (Romans 8:11). When a person returns to his sinful lifestyle after knowing the Lord, then he is worse off than in the beginning.

This happened to me. My second wife and I were serving the Lord by going to senior centers and I was giving a message and reading the Bible to them. She was singing unto the Lord for them. I had been a builder at this point and would travel to different Christian organizations and help them put up buildings or remodeling and striving to do whatever I could for the Lord. We had joined and became members in a church, and I taught Sunday school for a short time. Then I went to Bible college for a while. I just desired to serve the Lord in any way I could. I would witness to people and help them out in any way I could. After some years of steadily walking as upright as I could in this flesh and blood then I fell. My wife and I started drinking, going out, and doing the wrong things which eventually led me to jail again. This caused us to separate which led to a divorce in later times. satan looks to devour whom he may. (1 Peter 5:8).

At this point we were separated when I came across one of my brothers at a four-way stop and noticed he was pointing at me. I stopped the vehicle and rolled down my window as he started toward me. Little did I know he was angry with me and he opened

the door and grabbed me out of the van. At this point I had a blackout and was unaware of reality. I thought that we had wrestled around on the pavement in the middle of the intersection and I was on top of him choking him. I realized that this was wrong and let him go. Then I started following him to apologize and talk to him. I kept seeing his brake lights come on and eventually we ended up into an accident. In all reality the story didn't go like that at all.

At this point satan just had me wrapped around his pinky once again from falling away from the Lord. The truth and fact of the matter is he did pull me out of the vehicle, and we wrestled on the road but some people passing by stopped and pulled me off him. After which point, we were in a high-speed chase for about 5 miles before having a bad wreck. Every time I would see his brake lights, he was slowing down for curves and I would ram him with my vehicle. Every time his vehicle got up to a hundred miles per hour it would shut down and I would ram him with my vehicle. This put so many people in danger from the reckless driving and we ended up running off the road and both of us flipped our vehicles over several times. The next thing I knew, I didn't even realize I had been in the accident, only that I was walking through the woods with a dislocated shoulder. I wasn't sure what happened or where I was. Thank God my brother and his wife we're not seriously injured. I spent time in jail waiting for this case to get dismissed, luckily my brother knew that I was not in my right frame of mind. The charges were dropped in severity and I was released from jail.

Now, I thank the Lord that no one was hurt and that we made it through this night. This was another incident in which I had no regard for my own life, my brother's, his wife's, or for that matter just absolutely nobody. Anybody could have gotten in the way and they possibly would have been killed. Fortunately, the love of the Lord was with me once again and no one was seriously injured aside from me. It wasn't my time as the Lord continued long-suffering and patiently waiting for me to come to the point that I am at this stage in my life. He has pulled off another miraculous event that I have made it through.

So, from this experience I do fully believe that when a Christian walks according to Gods will and falls away, then they are in danger of having a terrible time. My roots as a Christian once again was not planted deeply into good soil and satan come along and uprooted me. So, as I know now it is our solemn duty to follow the leadership and guidance of the holy Spirit that dwells within us. (Matthew 12:43-45). After this horrific accident I sought after the Lord fervently and it was a total of two years that I was not in the Lord's will. I once again cried out unto the Lord our mediator Jesus Christ. (1 Timothy 2:5). I have been forgiven through His blood that was shed for me on the cross of Calvary. (Colossians 1:14).

Once again people, it is never too late to call upon the Lord and repent with a true heart for the forgiveness of our sins. He will separate them as far as the east is from the west. (Psalms 103:12). He is just to forgive us, and loving to hold it not against us, so therefore we must look directly toward Him for our leadership and guidance. Once we are stamped with the seal of the holy Spirit we are saved by God's grace through the blood of Jesus Christ at Calvary for all eternity. Now we need to act accordingly and do what the Lord would lead us and guide us to do to help glorify His kingdom.

(Jeremiah 3:22) *Return, ye backsliding children, and I will heal your backslidings. Behold, we come unto Thee; for Thou art the Lord our God.*

CHAPTER 3

The Old Man is Dead

The Bible talks about many times and many places where after we accept Jesus as our Lord and Savior, then we became a new creature. **(Psalms 66:19)**

*But verily God hath heard me; He hath attended to the voice of my prayer. * We must bury the old man and let Christ live through us. I have seen and have been a partaker in the past of people wanting to throw out the life jacket to the old man and try to help him stay alive. I now know that we must bury the old man and all his ways. **(Romans 6:6) *Knowing this, that our old man is crucified with Him, that the body of sin might be destroyed, that henceforth we should not serve sin.*** It doesn't matter who is involved, or what the situation is but one way or another we have to dispel the acting's, actions, and words from the old man.

Once we become a new creature in Christ, then we should not live by our sinful nature but adhere to what the Spirit convicts us to do. We must always pray and meditate on what the Spirit, would have us to do. If we fervently seek Him to lead us in our lives, our actions, thoughts, and words then we will be more blessed by the Lord as we are doing the right thing instead of doing the wrong thing. The Lord tells us that He will give us the words to say and that we don't need to think before we get there about what we are to say as it will be given unto us at the proper time.

(Luke 12:12). We must rely wholly upon the Lord to give us the words to say as He leads us and guides us when we come across certain situations that we need to speak boldly of the things concerning the Lord. Standing on His word, His promises, quench not the Spirit, but to deliver what He would have us to say. In this flesh and blood, we are weak and feeble and must rely upon the Lord. Sometimes we are put in the position that we feel embarrassed, don't want to hurt another person's feelings, we might think that it is not very important, or just simply don't want to do what we are led to do by the Spirit. We must immediately dismiss this as satan will try to veer and steer our words and actions from following Christ. We must only follow God and His guiding Spirit and not swerve off the straight and narrow path as satan will try to lead us down the wide path toward hells fire, therefore we cannot serve two master's. (Matthew 6:24). Water baptism is a public confession of the death and burial of the old man, the resurrection of the new creature in Christ, and serving the Lord as His children. After we confess Jesus as our Lord and Savior, it is the goal and should be the upmost important thing in a Christian's life to follow the will of God for our lives.

The Bible tells us not to sit in the seat of sinners and participate in the sins that they try to bring or bestow upon us. (Psalms 1:1). If we come across one of these situations, we must dismiss them immediately and continue forth and walk in an upright manner. Myself, I have an associate that works with me a little bit and he occasionally wants to talk about dirty jokes and jesting; I just ignore him and go on with a different conversation. (Ephesians 5:4). If I was being a participant in this action or I appealed to this person that their joke was funny, then I would be out of the way. The Bible tells us to let our light shine before man, not our light but the light of the Spirit dwelling within us. We must always walk according to the principles of the word of God. By acting and waking in this manner it is influential to other Christians and to the lost people. (Matthew 7:16).

We can all sit here and read the Bible, study it, and see so many ways where one is at fault. The most important thing is that a Christian is to evaluate his own soul, to renew his mind on a daily basis, and to follow the Spirit of the Lord. The renewing of one's mind is a daily thing. This don't just happen when we give our lives to the Lord after He calls us unto Himself. The renewing of our mind is a daily walk with Jesus. (Romans

2:1-2). As we enter many battles and spiritual warfares, throughout the day then we are to renew our minds accordingly as we seek the guidance and the strength of the Holy Spirit that dwells within us. We can't do this alone. (John 15:5). We all fall short on our walk every day. It is just a fact and if someone were to say they don't sin, that person is a liar. (1 John 1:8). So, the truth in God's word tells me that we sin every day. This sin is brought on at times and most every time that we go through spiritual warfare. Just a wrongful thought is a sin. (Proverbs 24:9-10). But to willingly sin is to act upon what satan is leading us to do, rather than relying on the correction of our Lord. We are to call on the name of the Lord and He will give us the strength to fight off the wiles of satan. (Ephesians 6:11). As we have the armor of God which includes the shield of faith then it will deflect the fiery darts of satan which come upon us daily. (Ephesians 6:16). When it is all said and done then it will just be one person standing before our Lord, our Heavenly Father, the creator of the universe. So, when it's time to stand in front of the judgment then you're going to be there alone. You won't be there with the sinner that you have participated in with their actions.

As we walk through this life there are so many spiritual battles that we must face and overcome and its only by the strength of the Lord that we can do this. His Spirit that dwells within every believer is stronger than the world. (John 16:33). If we look to Him, He will lead us and guide our paths and show us the correct way. So, back to the thought that it is easy to point out people's flaws, but is this opinionated of yourself or is this of the Lord by His holy word? So, when it's all said and done everyone will stand in front of Jesus Christ and will confess that he is Lord and Savior, the All Mighty God. (Romans 14:11). When we confess Jesus as our Lord and Savior, when He calls us unto Himself, then we will be accepted into heaven where he has gone to prepare a place. (John 14:2-3).

Myself personally, I would like to know at any time if I am talking out of the way, acting, or reacting out of the way concerning my words or actions toward someone or something. This cannot be an opinion as it doesn't matter to me about people's opinions when they're trying to correct me unless it is biblical and it it's coming from the word of God. The word of the Lord tells me that he is no respect of person.

(Romans 2:11). It is our duty to love our neighbor, but we don't have to like what they say or do. Simply put, everyone deserves common courtesy. There has been a question asked by many in different situations as they walk this path thinking about the right way to do so. What would Jesus do? That simply is the best question we could ask ourselves and the answer that dwells within us, Jesus has sent us a helper that will lead and guide us into all truth. (John 16:13). So, God has given us the Word, the Holy Bible, His love letter, that we should walk as Christ like as possible in this sinful flesh and blood. The Bible tells us that we should not judge unless we be judged. (Matthew 7:1). So, as we walk our walk of faith, then we must not look down upon others in different lowly circumstances or any other situations. We must not look at what they need or what they need to be doing but rather; how can we help them or what should we be doing as Christians? We are instructed to help those in need and to do unto others as we would have done unto us. (Matthew 7:12). So, we must pray to the Almighty God that He can help us keep an open mind and not look down upon others but rather pray for them. At all times the Bible, the instruction manual for walking this earth, tells us to listen quickly and be slow to speak and slow to anger. (James 1:19). This is the will of the Lord. As we trust and obey His word and His will for our lives through the guidance of the Holy Spirit, then we must let our light shine, not our light but the Lords light. (Matthew 5:16). Then we won't look at other peoples flaws but rather evaluate our on actions and thoughts. Self- examination is very important for a successful Christian. The Bible tells us to remove the log in our own eye before looking at the splinter in another's eye. (Matthew 7:3).

Within us having the Spirit that dwells within every believer, there is knowledge to all right and wrong.

We must just keep our minds and our hearts open unto the leadership of the Spirit so that we can follow the right path. For broad is the path to destruction and narrow is the path to everlasting joy, peace, and happiness. **(Matthew 7:13-14) *Enter ye in at the strait gate: for wide is the gate, and broad is the way, that leadeth to destruction, and many there be which go in thereat: 14 Because strait is the gate, and narrow is the way, which leadeth unto life, and few there be that find it.***

I so desire to have tunnel vision unto my Lord. I must focus on Him, and what He would do. Then this will bring me to my Creator, my Master, my loving Father at the end of this walk in the flesh and blood. Oh, what a day that will be, a day for rejoicing I see.

So, I do have a word I need to share concerning putting off the old man. Showing that he has been buried and a new creature walking in the likeness of the Lord as close as I can in this flesh and blood has prevailed. There is by no means that I can do this alone (John 15:5), the only way that this is possible is through the strength of the Lord's Spirit. I now look to my Lord for leadership and guidance for all things. (Philippians 4:13). There have been so many different events that has happened since I started truly following my Lord and Savior. I push off all evil through the power of His holy Spirit that dwells within me. I can only say it straight, meaning that I communicate only with truth and honesty. (Matthew 5:37). I follow as closely as I can to what the Bible tells me to do, which all comes from knowing Jesus as my Lord and Savior and having the holy Spirit dwell within me. He will lead and guide my path as I trod this earth.

(Galatians 3:6-27) *For ye are all the children of God by faith in Christ Jesus.* 27 *For as many of you as have been baptized into Christ have put on Christ.*

(Colossians 2:12-13) *Buried with Him in baptism, wherein also ye are risen with Him through the faith of the operation of God, who hath raised Him from the dead.* 13 *And you, being dead in your sins and the uncircumcision of your flesh, hath He quickened together with Him, having forgiven you all trespasses;*

CHAPTER 4

2ⁿᵈ Testimony

(Luke 3:16) *John answered, saying unto them all, I indeed baptize you with water; but one mightier than I cometh, the latchet of whose shoes I am not worthy to unloose: He shall baptize you with the Holy Ghost and with fire:*

(John 16:8) *And when He is come, He will reprove the world of sin, and of righteousness, and of judgment:*

After the crucifixion of our Lord Jesus Christ, then the holy Spirit comes to dwell within every believer. The holy Spirit is to lead, guide, and show us the path we must trod. The Spirit that dwells within us also leads us into all truth and can help us overcome our sinful nature. **(John 16:13).* Howbeit when He, the Spirit of truth, is come, He will guide you into all truth: for He shall not speak of himself; but whatsoever He shall hear, that shall He speak: and He will shew you things to come.***

(1 Thessalonians 5:19). *Quench not the Spirit. *

When God guides and convicts us through His Spirit then we need to react. Listening to the guidance of the Holy Spirit is the best path that we can follow as He wants the best for us. Our heavenly Father would want us to have the best and all that He can give us and the only way that we can receive this is to follow Him and His holy Spirit. If we dampen His Spirit, then it would be as a flame of a fire that don't have enough oxygen or air to burn bright or hot. I can refer and compare to God's holy Spirit as the flame of a candle. When we don't heed to what the Spirit would have us to do, then we are quenching the Spirit.

The Bible clearly tells us quench not the Spirit and we should be following Him. As we quench the Spirit and turn our backs on what the Lord would have us to do, then we are shunning His will for our lives. This will dampen the draw of the Spirit and the strength of God from us. God loves us so much that He gave us freedom of choice. So, as we go through life making all our own decisions and not listening to the guidance of the holy Spirit, then we are quenching the Spirit.

We are putting out the Spirit. We are not letting the Spirit work in our lives.

This is like taking oxygen away from a flame of a candle or fire. The fire starts to dampen and dim down. There comes a point to a fire that when all the oxygen is removed from the flame it will go out.

Luckily, that isn't the result with the holy Spirit's fire for us because, once we are sealed by the Spirit then we are always His. He will stay with us forevermore.

But as we continually quench the Spirit when He guides us, then He becomes more distant from our lives and our decisions. After quenching the Spirit for so long it is called grieving the Spirit. Grieving the Spirit makes Him sorrowful and we are just continually not listening to His guidance as we go about our own way. It is not good to make our heavenly Father sorrowful. We will end up making the wrong decisions for our lives. This saddens Him because we are headed for trouble and disaster when we are trying to rely upon our own decisions.

This will bring about turmoil to the Christian as it did pertaining to my life. I was supposed to quit smoking cigarettes and I felt convicted over smoking them but never stopped. I tried and then I always went back to them. This took place over a two-year term and the Spirit would only convict me of smoking. If we don't take the first step, then we can't take the second step and I was not listening to the directions of what the Lord was telling me.

So, then I never gained any more spiritual growth. Very sad to do to ourselves because we can do nothing on our own without the leadership and guidance of the Lord. (John15:5). As I went through my days I would still pray to God and I would go to church occasionally but not like I was before. This brought further distance from the Lord by my actions of disobedience and I continued to go down the wrong path once again.

I started drinking heavy and started dating other girls and just living unrighteous. I removed the Lord from my life and rejected His guiding Spirit. Without the Lord being in my life then this allowed satan to take back control. Once again, we cannot serve two masters. (Matthew 6:24). Somehow through the deception of satan I had started serving him once again.

Through this unrighteous living, I had found myself incarcerated once again. I was looking at five life sentence charges and waiting for my jury trial. When I was arrested, I cried out unto the Lord as I sat in that cold dingy jail cell with all this time I was facing. I cried out to the Lord I say. I had sinned against the Lord and quenched His Spirit for two years straight.

I did not hear or feel the Spirit of God comforting me when I was calling to Him. I cried unto the Lord for two weeks before I finally felt his arms wrap around me with comfort. **(Psalms 40:1) *I waited patiently for the LORD; and He inclined unto me and heard my cry. *** It was the absolute scariest situation I had ever been in during my entire life. I felt as if I lost my salvation and was headed straight to hell. After I felt the comforting arms of our Lord and Saviors Spirit, then life was okay again. I was still in jail looking at the rest of my life in prison, but I had the Spirit of God within me.

As the three and a half months of my incarceration evolved, then I drew closer unto the Spirit of God. He drew closer to me through studying His word and a lot of meditation. **(Acts 3:19). *Repent ye therefore, and be converted, that your sins may be blotted out, when the times of refreshing shall come from the presence of the Lord;*** During this time of my incarceration and drawing closer unto the Lord I asked forgiveness and repented with a true heart. Our loving, just, and kind Father that we have, forgave me. He has set my feet upon solid ground once again. (Psalms 40:2).

As I was living my life the way I chose to and ran from the Lord's word then he was still patiently waiting for me. That doesn't mean there won't be disciplinary actions that I must receive from the Lord. It just means that the Lord cares for me and loves me. **(Hebrews 12:5-11)**. **And ye have forgotten the exhortation which speaketh unto you as unto children, My son, despise not thou the chastening of the Lord, nor faint when thou art rebuked of Him:*

6 For whom the Lord loveth He chasteneth, and scourgeth every son whom He receiveth.

7 If ye endure chastening, God dealeth with you as with sons; for what son is he whom the father chasteneth not?

8 But if ye be without chastisement, whereof all are partakers, then are ye bastards, and not sons.

9 Furthermore we have had fathers of our flesh which corrected us, and we gave them reverence: shall we not much rather be in subjection unto the Father of spirits, and live?

10 For they verily for a few days chastened us after their own pleasure; but He for our profit, that we might be partakers of His holiness.

11 Now no chastening for the present seemeth to be joyous, but grievous: nevertheless afterward it yieldeth the peaceable fruit of righteousness unto them which are exercised thereby.*

This brings about the story of Jonah into my mind. Jonah was instructed by the Lord to go to the people of the great city of Nineveh and preach. Jonah did not want to go to the great city of Nineveh because they were not friends, they were enemies. So, Jonah disregarded what the Lord had said and started traveling away from the Lord. Jonah once again disregarded what the Lord had said and boarded a ship. Ultimately, the ship was going through stormy weather and the crew found out that Jonah was the cause of these storms. They threw Jonah into the waters and the storm was calm.

The Lord brought a big fish to swallow Jonah, and he stayed in the belly of Hell away from the Lord for three days. He cried out unto the Lord and after three days the Lord heard him and had the big fish spew him out on the shore. After this the Lord once again instructed Jonah to go preach to the great city of Nineveh so these people shall be saved. Jonah then went on his way to Nineveh and a great number of people was saved.

Ultimately, when we disobey the Lord and quench His Spirit, this will bring about sorrow unto Him. The Lord is leading and guiding us unto His lost children that we may witness to them. We must plant, seed and water to help His kingdom grow that we can come to his lost children in time of accordance. So, when we don't follow the instructions of what the Lord would have us to do by the guiding of His Spirit, then it's not just hurting ourselves. We are hurting others whose paths we are supposed to cross. Simply put, quench not the Spirit.

The chastening hand of the Lord was stern and that is what I needed in my life. This finalized my disobedience unto the Lord. I only desire to help glorify His kingdom, and I will do it at any cost no matter any person or any reason that stands in the way. My only desire, my number one goal in life, is to be used as a sharp tool to enhance and glorify the kingdom of God. I am his bond servant and I love my Lord and Savior Jesus Christ who has saved me through His blood and through God's grace.

It might seem like a long time spending three and a half months incarcerated for accusations brought against me, but ultimately, this was the best thing that could have happened in my life. I lost everything I had, a cabin and 5 acres, a handful friends that were not friends, and everything else materialistic that I owned. Seek ye first the kingdom of heaven and all else will follow. **(John 14:16-21) *And I will pray the Father, and He shall give you another Comforter, that He may abide with you for ever; 17 Even the Spirit of truth; whom the world cannot receive, because it seeth Him not, neither knoweth Him: but ye know Him; for He dwelleth with you, and shall be in you. 18 I will not leave you comfortless: I will come to you. 19 Yet a little while, and the world seeth Me no more; but ye see me: because I live, ye shall live also. 20 At that day ye shall know that I am in My Father, and ye in Me, and I in you. 21 He that hath My commandments, and keepeth them, he it is that loveth Me: and he that loveth Me shall be loved of my Father, and I will love him, and will manifest Myself to him.***

After the chastening of the Lord and me full heartedly repenting and crying out unto the Lord, then my Christian walk was straightened out. During my trials and tribulations, I have grown so much and gathered so much wisdom from the Lord. The Bible tells me that when we go through hard times as what I went through during my incarceration, then we know the Lord is walking beside us. (Hebrews 13:5-6). As we do go through these hard times then we should be happy that we are learning something during them.

Always know that everything happens for the good of those that love the Lord. (Romans 8:28).

I no longer believe in coincidence. I don't believe in bad karma or good karma. I believe in chastisement and blessings from the Lord. I don't believe in bad luck or good luck; I believe that what comes around goes around. We should treat others how we want to be treated. **(Romans 12:12).**

*Rejoicing in hope; patient in tribulation; continuing instant in prayer; *

The Bible continues to tell us to pray without ceasing. (1st Thessalonians 5:17). I think we should always be praying all day long. Giving thanks unto the Lord for everything that we have and for everything that we don't have, because if we want it and we don't have it then there is probably a reason. The Lord will supply us with everything that we need and everything we desire that is in His will for our lives. The things that we can handle that He would have us to have. (Romans 8:28). Everyone has gifts that the Lord gives unto them. (Romans 12:6).

All these gifts are varying and none the same, as the complete body needs all the different parts to function. Our fingers have different functions than our toes and our arms have different functions from our legs. As everything is put together then we have a complete functioning body. The body of Christ is the One True Church. (Colossians 1:18). Different Christians are called according to their gifts and what they should be doing in the body of Christ to make it a functioning unit. (1 Corinthians 12:12). Everyone has a purpose in God's plan.

I lean solely on the Lord during my trials and tribulations. So, during my incarceration I knew that everything would work out to the glorification of our Lord and Savior. I'm here to share my testimony with everyone and anyone that will listen. I just want to plant, seed, and water for our Lord. My number one goal in life, my most fervent prayer is that the Lord uses me according to His purpose for the best that I can be to help uplift His name and glorify His Kingdom. I must do this full heartedly as this feels what I must do.

The Lord has delivered me from Hell, the separation that I felt during my disobedience toward Him. Hell is a separation from the Lord. The Lord blesses me every day, all day long. I can't even keep up with my blessings. If I was to give thanks for every blessing of all day then, I would have time for nothing but to say thank you Lord, thank you Lord, thank you Lord continually all day. This is a true statement. The Lord lifted me up from such a deep dark dingy place and He has set my feet upon the solid rock again. I thank you Lord. (Psalms 40:2). I thank you Lord for establishing my ways and helping my mind to be straight and to give me tunnel vision that leads directly toward you. Lord let all my actions and all my words speak of you. Father let me be a light unto the lost and let me be a testimony unto you.

I no longer desire to turn back and look at the mess that I come from as Lot's wife did. She was turned into a pillar of salt for her disobedience. The Lord simply told them don't turn back, don't look back, to run away from this mess and Lot's wife looked back and was instantly turned into a pillar of salt. In my testimony earlier I talked about returning to my nasty ways as the dog returns to its vomit and the pig returns to the miry pit. (2 Peter 2:22).

Now the Lord has given me strength and opened my eyes and I have gained so much wisdom from Him that I will never turn my back on Him again.

I will always keep His vision in my sight. Thank you, Lord, for the acknowledgement that I cannot do nothing without you. (John15:5). I absolutely will make the wrong decisions in everything I do unless I ask the Lord and He directs me. **(Luke 9:62) *And Jesus said unto him, No man, having put his hand to the plough, and looking back, is fit for the kingdom of God.*** The Lord is long-suffering with His children and when He starts a work in us then He will finish it no matter what it takes or how long. **(Philippians 1:6) *Being confident of this very thing, that He which hath begun a good work in you will perform it until the day of Jesus Christ: ***

I choose only to follow the Lord's Spirit. I do not desire to get snared into the wiles of satan anymore. I carry the Lords armor with me that I might withstand the fiery darts of satan and overcome all my spiritual warfare's through the strength of the Lord. (Ephesians 6:11). We cannot choose to walk with the Lord and then in the next breath do something that the Lord would not have us to do. We must only serve the Lord or deny our Savior Jesus Christ which will send us straight to hell's fire for all eternity, suffering for all eternity apart from God. (Matthew 6:24). I didn't understand this at one point in my life. I was lost and undone for the first 28 years of my life and always made the wrong decisions. I made the worst decisions a person can make.

I was the vilest sinner there could be and how shameful I was when I first was called to the Lord and repented for all my sins. I named every one of my sins, one by one, and asked for forgiveness. Once we ask for forgiveness for our sins from the Lord then they are separated as far from the east is to the west. (Psalms 103:12). I am so thankful to God for helping me get through all the stages of my life that I am at right now.

I can see my prayers coming true every one of them that I plead for. I see them all unfold, and I am thankful for this. My fervent prayer was for a good girl to stand beside me and I have received her. She is here and the Lord has sent her to help me for the rest of my life. We choose to serve God together and put His will first and foremost in our lives as we finish writing this book. We look forward to the continuing guidance of our Lord. Thank you Father, in Jesus name.

Chapter 5

Quench Not the Spirit

1 Thessalonians 5:19 *Quench not the Spirit.*

This verse has become one of the most important words in God's Bible to me. This is what makes the Christian walk possible. This is what makes our paths straight. This is what makes it possible to please God. This is what makes it possible to find the center of God's will for our lives. To quench not the Spirit means listening to God's holy Spirit that dwells within every Christian.

As we walk upon this earth in this flesh and blood, it should be our greatest desire to have spiritual growth and desire to draw closer to God. It is our duty and should be our number one goal in life to have spiritual growth daily. Spiritual growth comes from studying our Bible, prayer, meditation, and being led by the holy Spirit. As we are led by the holy Spirit and continue in God's will for our lives, then we see more of our prayers being answered in accordance to how we ask them. Seeing our prayers answered should absolutely increase our faith in God that He is there answering our prayers and He is a rewarder of them that diligently seek Him. (Hebrews 11:6).

As our prayers are answered and our faith is increased then this should draw us closer to being more like Christ, which comes through spiritual growth. Spiritual growth is becoming more Christ-like and desiring to be in the absolute center of God's will for our lives. As we grow spiritually then we can count on the promises of God that they will hold true and He will sustain, lead, and guide us through all our trials and tribulations. He told us to take His yoke for this is the easy way. (Matthew 11:30). When we do this our spiritual growth enhances more and more becoming more Christ-like as we are new creature's in Christ, and we become stronger in the Lord. (Ephesians 6:10).

All these, factor into an amazing comfortable life no matter what valley is the deepest, darkest that we come across or any situations or circumstances that satan tries to entice us with. We will be strong enough to overcome all obstacles that satan puts in our paths calling upon the name of the Lord. (Psalms 50:15). **(Philippians 1:6); *Being confident of this very thing, that He which hath begun a good work in you will complete it until the day of Jesus Christ:*** When the Spirit of God called us and we accepted God's grace through faith in Jesus for our salvation through the atonement of his blood then God began to work on us. (Romans 3:25).

We have a loving, kind, long-suffering, forgiving, and just God that we serve. Our heavenly Father is love; God is love. (1 John 4:8). On the other hand, He expects His children to behave. As a dad chastises his children for doing wrong, the Lord will also chastise us. We as Christians are dealt with accordingly when we do not listen to His Spirit leading us. So, this work that the Lord started in us will be completed after we accept Jesus as our Lord and Savior. The Bible tells us don't look down upon the chastening hand of the Lord. (Proverbs 3:11).

For it is a blessing to be chastened by the Lord as this shows His love toward us and for us and that we are ignoring His leadership and guidance in our lives. So, as Christ started this work in us, He will finish it and we are sealed until the day of redemption when Jesus comes to gather His church by the holy Spirit we are sealed. (Ephesians 1:13). We have trusted Christ to save us, then we must trust Him to lead and guide us through life's daily problems. This is our bond with the almighty God, the master of the universe, the Lord of lords and creator of all. We have intimate relations with God through the holy Spirit from the crucifixion of His only begotten son Jesus Christ. (John 3:16).

So, as we rely on the Spirit to lead us and guide us each day after we accept Him, it is our Christian duty to follow the Spirit, quench not the Spirit. (1 Thessalonians 5:19). This means to listen as we are told and to trust and obey. This is a main source of our Christian growth drawing nearer to God through His Spirit, through prayer and meditation. These are all factors of our Christian growth, our spiritual growth. We must make every effort to add to our faith and knowledge always seeking the Lord's guidance. This will bring a productive lifestyle to all Christians who seek Him.

Our second great Commandment that Jesus spoke when He walked this earth is love thy neighbor as thyself. (Matthew 22:39). This will complete a Christians walk and bring so much peace to one's mind and soul if you can follow this second great commandment. God is love, so loving our neighbor is something we must do. To love our neighbor is to show him courtesy and treat him as we would want to be treated ourselves. To love our neighbor is to help one another. To love our neighbor is to not take any negative actions or wrongdoing towards them. To love our neighbor completes our Christian walk with Christ. If we can grab onto this, it will bring great spiritual growth.

As Christians we should know that we wrestle not against flesh and blood but against principalities and dark powers of this world. (Ephesians 6:12). If we can know, truly know, that a fellow human being is being led, tricked, deceived, or manipulated into doing wrong by satan then we can overcome our anger or dislike for this person. This will also increase our spiritual growth incredibly. Jesus tells us in **(John 15:4:5) * Abide in Me, and I in you. As the branch cannot bear fruit of itself, except it abide in the vine; no more can ye, except ye abide in me. I am the vine, ye are the branches: He that abideth in Me, and I in him, the same bringeth forth much fruit: for without Me you can do nothing. ***

Through Jesus when we are led by the Holy Spirit, we have spiritual growth and become more like Christ.

Love shall abound for Christians. The Bible says they will know us by our fruits. (Matthew 7:16). When we look through the scripture, we find that we have eternal life and that we are to testify of the Lord.

(John 5:39). As we let our light shine, the Bible says don't keep it under a basket. (Matthew 5:15). But rather let others see Christ through us as we are new creatures in Christ. (2 Corinthians 5:17). Then others should be able to recognize us by this, by our actions, and by our words living in the Lord's will. This will bring us to Him for all eternity. Jesus says in my Father's house there are many mansions, if it was not so I would have told you. (John 14:2).

As we walk this earth in this natural body it is one day to be returned to the earth as the dust from where it was formed. (Ecclesiastes 12:7). So, we must run the good race to reach our goal to the point of spending all eternity with our heavenly Father. As we walk in this natural flesh, we will come across different trials and tribulations. (Romans 5:3). We go through different trials so that we can have spiritual growth; (Hebrews 12:7) tells us to endure hardships as disciplined by God while He is treating us as sons.

We won't like being disciplined as does any child, but as we all know it brings out a better mannerism for the child and helps the child grow into a better person.

This is the Lord's desire for us to become like- minded with Christ and have spiritual growth throughout our walk on this earth. When we undergo the chastening of the Lord, we go through trials, tribulations, and hardships that brings spiritual growth and draws us nearer to Christ. After a spell when we get through the valley, the deep dark miry pits we often come into, then we can look unto the Lord and give Him the glory for bringing us fourth out of this pit. The chastening of the Lord is good because if we are being disciplined then we surely do need it. As I have been chastened by the Lord it brought me closer to God and my Christian walk became stronger and my spirit was growing. I was studying, praying, meditating, and looking fully to the Lord for His comfort, leadership, and guidance.

As we grow spiritually just like children grow, as they learn through discipline and guidance from their parents, we also grow through our heavenly Father's leadership and guidance. This will mean less chastisement and more peace being brought upon us. As we continue to seek God's leadership and continue to grow closer to His spirit then we have a deeper desire to understand His word, His holy word, the Bible, it is our instruction manual for being here in this human body. It will lead us to the heavenly Father one day. When we first are called by the Spirit and accept Jesus as our Lord and Savior then we are babes in Christ. This means that we are given milk, which is His word for our spiritual growth and as a baby the more milk that is given unto this child, the more it will grow. After a spell we will get into a meatier substance and our studies will become deeper and this is all part of our spiritual growth. (1 Corinthians 3:2).

God will give us wisdom if we ask and open His word up to us to show us the way He would have us to go, the path that we must trod. The more we open ourselves up unto the Spirit of God the easier it is for Him to lead us and the more abundantly our spirit will become one with His and we will grow in the Lord.

For it was God that gave his only begotten Son, Jesus Christ, that all that believe upon Him shall be saved. (Acts 16:31).

Everyone who believes that Jesus is Lord, that He died for our sins on the cross, rose again the third day and now sits on the right hand of the Father shall be saved. His Spirit dwells within us, leads us, and guides us. He shows us the path that we must trod. He tells us what to do at specific times in our lives.

We must trust and obey the word of God and the Spirit of God because otherwise we cannot please Him. Then we are not doing the right thing according to God's will.

We can't ask why He is leading and guiding us here because His overall perfect plan is more than we can understand and more than we can comprehend. God knows all, He is all knowing. (Hebrews 4:13). As we walk here in this flesh and blood we are in a weak state and the only way we can make it through this is by looking unto the Lord and hanging on His promises. Jesus, before He left and ascended told us that He will send the comforter, this comforter is His holy Spirit that dwells within us.

Our bodies are the living temple of the great God, the only God. We cannot see God but, we can most assuredly talk to Him and have a relationship with Him through His Spirit, through prayer, meditation, and desire. The Spirit will lead and guide us, and the path may seem hard and we might not want to do what we should be doing but we must act upon the guidance of our Lord. We must be obedient and trust the direction we are being led by the Spirit. (Romans 8:12). If we do not listen to the Spirit or be led to do accordingly, then this could hinder the Lord in using us as a tool to glorify His kingdom. Therefore, I quench not the Spirit. (1Thessalonians 5:19). It is a decision to follow the Lord and it is a lifestyle to quench not the Spirit. We have His living word, the Bible, as an instruction manual to figure out the problems and the directions of our lives. God speaks through His word.

God speaks to us in prayer and meditation. God speaks to us, leads us, and guides us through His Holy Spirit. When we know the Spirit of God is leading us towards an action or words, then we must stand up and do what the Lord would have us to do. There is a point that we must discern the spirits. When we become strong satan just can't scream at us anymore because we won't act upon his evil desires.

He must whisper and make it sound as if the Lord is wanting us to do hi evil desires. This is spiritual discernment. (1 John 4:1). As we draw closer to God and we are walking in the center of His will then we are strengthened by His Spirit and led to do things that the Lord would have us to do. Most assuredly we can know that anything good that comes to our minds, is not of satan. There is a time that we must pray, meditate, and look for further instructions from the Lord because satan is being gentle in trying to deceive us that are strong and are knowledgeable in God's word.

For those that are not knowledgeable in God's word then satan don't have to be as careful. Now being a carnivore of the Lord, satan must try to whisper to me, and I immediately turn to the Spirit of the Lord for discernment and victory over the whiles of the devil. Once again, the most important verse in my Christian walk now is **(1 Thessalonians 5:19**

Quench not the Spirit). This will put me in the place where I need to be, and this will give me the actions that I need to take.

This will lead me to the place, the destination of where I need to be so that I might be of help planting a seed or watering a seed that the Lord will pluck when the fruit is ready. The Lord says to always be ready in His word. (1 Peter 3:15). If we as Christians quench the Spirit, then we are putting a kink in God's perfect plan. God has given us the freedom of choice and the free will that we have. So, if we quench the Spirit and do not listen to what God would have us to do, we can open His holy word and read about Jonah.

Jonah was a prophet of the Lord that was supposed to go preach to the great city of Nineveh so that many shall be saved, and the Spirit of God came on Jonah and directed him this way. Jonah made his own decision to quench the Spirit of God and not listen to what the Lord would have him to do. Jonah went off the other way. The long story short of it, he disobeyed God. Now, as we all know Jonah was swallowed by the great fish and during this time in the fish's belly, he was crying out to God from the belly of hell. Jonah cried unto the Lord and repented with fear and trembling for his wrongdoing and was willing to go the extra mile and listen to what the Lord would have him to do. Jonah cried out of the whale's belly and the Lord heard him. (Jonah 2:2).

The Lord had the great fish spit Jonah up on the shore and Jonah was able to complete God's mission for his life. Jonah went and preached to the great city of Nineveh and many were saved. I have quenched the Spirit. I was supposed to quit smoking for two years. I used to smoke cigarettes and they are very addicting, and satan had so many ways to grab onto me through them. The Lord had led me to know that I needed to quit smoking cigarettes and I quenched His Spirit for two years. I did not listen to the Spirit of God leading and guiding me that I should quit these cigarettes. I was still going to church and I was still praying but as I quenched the Spirit, I was separating myself from the relationship that I had with the Lord.

During this two-year span I quenched the Spirit, then satan was able to slip in and start whispering sweet nothings to me and it was drowning out the Spirit of God.

satan started to convince me that I wanted to go back to the worldly things and see how much fun it would be to have worldly desires in this natural flesh and blood. I became weak and was following satan once again. The Lord will not make us do anything, He wants us to choose Him and I fell out of fellowship with His Spirit. I quenched the Spirit. When we don't do what God would have us to do then we cannot know the next thing He wants us to do. We cannot get to second or third base and surely not home if we don't go to first base. So, there is a pattern to listening and being led by God's Spirit.

Quench not the Spirit, react and obey to what the Lord would lead us to do. The Lord's Spirit had become quite after I had dampened Him that dwelled inside of me. I was just listening to satan at this point a time. So, through my worldly desires God's Spirit was no longer in my grasp as I had denied him consistently and constantly for two years. After we continually quench the Lord's Spirit, this begins to grieve His Spirit. This makes the Lord very sorrowful and we know this is not good from the story of Noah. God was sorrowful when he looked at his creation and all the disobedience in those days. At first glance, satan's plan looks so luscious and so enticing that we want all these things. He doesn't show us the end of his plan which is death, destruction, sadness, misery, and eventually if you are led by satan, you die following him.

Now, you are living in hell for all eternity, being separated from the love of God, by your own decisions. So, just looking at the good, fun things that satan had led me to believe, then I found myself in such a lowly state, that I had nobody, I had nothing, my life was in shambles. I cried unto the Lord from the tiny little jail cell that I found myself in. I cried unto the Lord for two weeks straight, feeling not His Spirit, feeling not His comfort, feeling not His guidance, feeling not His Spirit that I had quenched for two years. I was scared! I was alone, confused, and lost. I no longer felt the joy of my salvation. (Psalms 51:12).

I continually cried unto the Lord and read His word from this little cold room. One day, the Lord wrapped his arms around me, and I started feeling His comforting arms embracing me once again. The Lord had returned the joy of my salvation. I was lost, scared, and alone when God reached down into the miry pit that I had willingly jumped into serving satan and denying the Spirit and He pulled me out. (Psalms 40:2). So, at this point I started and continued to look toward the Lord, studied His word, prayed, and meditated. I no longer quench the Spirit of the Lord and I never will again.

So, let us stay in the center of God's will. If we have accepted Jesus as our Lord and Savior, know that He was crucified for our sins, only His blood can atone for our sins, that He arose again on the third day and sits on the right hand of the Father, then we shall be saved. (Romans 8:34). Ultimately, when we as Christians come to know God and believe all these things, then we will be chastened by the Lord for our wrongdoings. (Hebrews 12:6).

We must all repent and Jesus will forgive us our sins. (Acts 3:19). When we quench the Spirit then we are disobedient children and must be chastened. When we quench the Spirit, we cannot take the next step toward being in the center of God's will. When we quench the Spirit, we miss out on blessings of the Lord because we are not in the right place, we are not in the right frame of mind, and we are not doing as what the Lord would have us to do.

I am truly blessed and happy in the Lord. I only have a desire to continue in the center of God's will because that's where I find peace and happiness. This is where all of God's children will find peace and happiness. Directly in the center of God's will for our lives. **(1 John 2:17). *And the world passeth away, and the lusts thereof: but he that doeth the will of God abideth for ever.***

CHAPTER 6

Thankfulness

1 Thessalonians 5:18 *In every thing give thanks: for this is the will of God in Christ Jesus concerning you.*

We have heard good versus evil all our lives; it has been good versus evil for all of time since the beginning of creation. Since the Garden of Eden. There's only two ways in this world, choices of master's to serve in this world. The Bible tells us that we cannot serve two masters. (Matthew 6:24). There is always a constant struggle of good versus evil. The Bible calls this spiritual warfare. There is a pull in the positive and in the negative direction in anything that we do in life. Being thankful is of the Lord, it is of good.

Being unthankful or ungrateful, is of satan, it is of evil. It is of the negative things of this world. It is our choice in life to defeat satan by putting off his fiery darts thrown at us by using the shield of faith, which God gives us to strengthen us as part of our body of armor. (Ephesians 6:16). If we adhere to what satan would have us to do, then we are losing this battle. Being ungrateful and unthankful for what the Lord has given us and done for us is so terrible. Being ungrateful and unthankful for what another brother gives us is also very terrible because we are supposed to do all things as unto the Lord. (Colossians 3:23).

Everything I do I get the Lord involved into it and He leads, guides, and corrects me. I fall at times but if I continually look for my heavenly Father to correct me and lift me back up then I am doing the best that I can living on this earth in this flesh and blood. If I don't look for His heavenly way, the righteous way, that He would have me to walk, then I am letting Him down. Lord, I just thank you for the privilege of prayer. Knowing that when I fervently look for you through meditation and prayer that you are there, that you are listening to my plea and my cry. **(1 John 5:14-15) * And this is the confidence that we have in Him, that if we ask any thing according to His will, He heareth you.**

15 And if we know that He hear us, whatsoever we ask, we know that we have the petitions that we desired of Him.*

It is so awesome that I can open a direct line to the almighty God, the creator of heaven and earth, the great I Am, my heavenly Father, so many more to be said but just overall my awesome Lord. I thank you that you listen to me when I talk to you. I thank you Lord that through my meditation through other people, and through your word Lord that you talk to me. I hear you so clearly Lord and I just strive to continue this open communication Father. Lord, I just can't do nothing without you and being able to meditate on your word and listen for your guidance through your holy Spirit that dwells within me, I thank you for this privilege.

Prayer is such a blessing that we all overlook at times. I just want you to remind me Lord through everything thick and thin, in the valleys and on the mountains, that you my Lord, my God are listening and just one word away. You are there when I need to call upon you Father, I thank you in Jesus precious name. I know Lord that you do hear all our prayers and that they are answered accordingly to what your will would be for our lives and that direct situation. (Philippians 4:9). I thank you for the unanswered prayers that I cannot understand but, later usually do see why they were not answered according to how I asked. I just strive to stay in the center of your will so that my prayers will be answered according to what you would have me to pray and want.

As I do know that you want the best for me while I'm walking in this flesh and blood and I am just so thankful. Thank you, Lord, that I can continually give you thanks and continually pray all day. (1 Thessalonians 5:18). At times I don't ask a blessing on my meals, but I always give thanks. Lord your word tells me that the prayers of a man that's walking uprightly as close as we can in your sight, that they are effective and that you do listen. I have been in the place and position where I have prayed unto you Father and I know that I wasn't doing the right thing Lord and I saw that if the prayers of a righteous man availeth much, then the prayers of a sinner does nothing. I thank you for this knowledge Lord and I just would like to impress it upon all that would listen to me. If we're praying and we don't believe, then it is not doing any good if we're not walking in a Christian like manner.

(James 5:16) *Confess your faults one to another, and pray one for another, that ye may be healed. The effectual fervent prayer of a righteous man availeth much.* Lord help me in Jesus name to become one that prays better. I know that you answer my prayers Lord, they can be answered yes, no or later according to which you see would be best for me. There are occasions Lord that I don't know exactly what to pray when someone is going through difficult times or what to say when someone don't understand why things are happening to them.

Lord all I can do is let them know that you're in charge and that all things happen for the good of those that love you Father. (Romans 8:28). Your word leads and guides us into the prayer that Jesus taught us as He walked on this earth which is our main prayer to follow. **(Matthew 6:9-13) *After this manner therefore pray ye: Our Father which art in heaven, Hallowed be Thy name. 10 Thy kingdom come. Thy will be done in earth, as it is in heaven.***

11 Give us this day our daily bread. 12 And forgive us our debts, as we forgive our debtors.

13 And lead us not into temptation but deliver us from evil: For Thine is the kingdom, and the power, and the glory, for ever. Amen. *

I see Father as your holy word was given to us accordingly that when my Lord and Savior Jesus Christ walked this earth then He was the perfect man and demonstrated in many situations of how Christians should act, live, and speak. I remember Jesus praying and wishing He didn't have to go through what was to come but, His prayer was not my will be done but your will Father. That's what I want out of my prayer life Lord. Because I know that my thoughts and my decisions will not get me anywhere but in trouble or in a bad situation. I need your guidance I cannot do anything on my own. (John 5:30).

Through the guidance of your holy Spirit I commit my prayers, knowing your holy Spirit will make grumblings for me to the Father when I do not know what to pray for. (Romans 8:26-27). I am thankful for this Father and I give you thanks in Jesus name. I know that my prayers are not just empty words and when my heart is into you so deeply as it is then you know what I desire and what I want in my life Lord. (Psalms 37:4). Father God I look to your Spirit always for the leadership and guidance in my life as I meditate in my prayer closet. (Matthew 6:6). I look unto you for answers. I have received answers directly from you in my meditation, so many answers from other Christians, from pastures where I hear you speak to me through them.

I feel, see, and hear your guidance even through the lost children Lord. This helps steer me from trouble and helps me to stay on track while I walk this path here on earth. I know through prayer and meditation that you will continually lead and guide me where I should walk, point my mind in the direction that I should think accordingly and touch my soul in a manner of what I should feel. Through my prayers I will always give you thanks and lift your name upon high, we're it belongs Lord. With you Father personally knowing my heart, and because of that I am very pleased. (Psalms 139:1-2).

Because, there is without a doubt that my most fervent prayer unto you Lord, that you use me for the glorification of your kingdom. No matter what you would have me to do Father, my whole life desires to stay in the center of your will and help your lost children along the way. **(James 5:20) * Let him know, that which converteth the sinner from the error of his way shall save a soul from death, and shall hide a multitude of sins.* I** just ask that you give me the words, the strength, the understanding, and the courage to react, speak, and deliver whatever it is that you would have me your faithful bondservant, to do in this flesh and blood. **(Ephesians 6:18-20) *Praying always with all prayer and supplication in the Spirit, and watching thereunto with all perseverance and supplication for all saints; 19 And for me, that utterance may be given unto me, that I may open my mouth boldly, to make known the mystery of the gospel, 20**

For which I am an ambassador in bonds: that therein I may speak boldly, as I ought to speak.*

I only desire to plant, seed, and water for your future Kingdom to come Lord. Use me, Father, in Jesus name I pray. The Lord tells us in **(Mark 11:24)**

*****Therefore I say unto you, what things so ever ye desire, when we pray, believe that ye receive them, and ye shall have them.*** These are words that lost people don't exactly understand. To fully understand this verse, one must be close to the Spirit of God, being led and given wisdom and knowledge of this verse is very special. When your eyes are opened unto this verse and the true meaning of this verse means exactly what it says. If we ask for something in prayer, then our heavenly Father will give it to us.

That is an absolute fact. But just to read that verse for someone that does not understand the word of God, they will take that generically and not too heart and deep within their soul. Meaning they could ask for just anything and the Lord will give it to them. **(James 4:3) *Ye ask, and receive not, because ye ask amiss, that ye may consume it upon your lusts. ***

This isn't true, when we pray as devout Christians then we are led by the Spirit of God and we would be praying for the things that we need and desire most that would be in the center of God's will for us to have. The closer we draw to the Spirit of God, then the more we will ask accordingly to what He would want us to have in our lives. As we draw closer to the Spirit of God, we will see our prayers develop just about exactly how we pray for things. Because when we draw closer to the Spirit of God and His Spirit draws closer unto us then we are becoming one spirit and want the same thing. The same thing from our prayer would be the same thing that the heavenly Father would want us to have while walking on this earth in this flesh and blood. Therefore, we must be walking uprightly and close to God to receive these things.

Because, as babes in Christ then we might not totally understand what the Lord would have us to do. But as we grow in our Christian walk; which is very important for us to develop into Christ like creatures that pray for things to enhance and glorify the kingdom of God through receiving blessings at the same time from our heavenly Father. Hence, this is a lot deeper than if you were to just read it, there is so much more into this verse of asking and you shall receive. As we grow in our prayer life and listen to what the Lord would have us to pray for and want us to have, we would have the best in our lives.

Then we start understanding more and our prayers become stronger as we draw closer to the holy Spirit. One of the hardest prayers to pray is, for someone that hates you, despises you, uses you or is your enemy. I have been in horrible situations due to false allegations and false witnesses and have had many enemies along my path in this life. When I was a babe in Christ I would pray for my enemies because the Bible tells me when I pray for my enemies that it will heap coals upon their heads. (Proverbs 25:22). This was not the right way to think and this was not for the right reason to pray for my enemies and those who despitefully used me.

During my Christian growth I have developed wisdom from the Lord that brought me to the realization that I need to pray for my enemies and people that use me wrongfully because they are lost and satan has a hold of them and they need to be saved. They need the Lord in their lives, and a true commitment unto Him so they do not go straight to hell. I now know to pray for people that are my enemies and I pray for them because I once was led by satan and was headed straight to hell. So, I fervently pray for my enemies and for people that do me wrong because it is not the flesh and blood that we wrestle against, it's the evil principalities and darkness of this world. (Ephesians 6:12). Once again, our enemies are not God's children that are lost being led by satan, but our enemies are evil spirits, satan, and darkness among this world. So, I implore all Christians to develop and learn to pray for their enemies as it has helped me so much in my Christian walk. Now I truly have the heart that my enemies would repent unto the Lord and be saved and not spend eternity in hell which was made for satan and his angels.

Once I learned this which falls under love. Once I learned to pray for my enemies and forgive them and realized it is satan who is leading them. My life became so much more peaceful. There is so much to learn from this, as now I do not become angry but just for a second when someone does me wrong and this brings about a peaceful easy feeling in my life. I am so thankful for the privilege of prayer that I may call upon the Lord immediately and ask for the strength of His Spirit to help fight the fiery darts of satan that he hurls at me when someone does me wrong. I can immediately through the strength of the spirit dismiss those thoughts. **(Matthew 5:44)** *But I say unto you, Love your enemies, bless them that curse you, do good to them that hate you, and pray for them which despitefully use you, and persecute you;* We must truly know that the Lord will listen to us and our every prayer and thought. So, we must continuously keep in our prayers that we grow with the Spirit that's leading and guiding us.

God's word is truth, God's word is real, God tells us in His holy word that He hears us when we lift our prayers to Him. **(Psalms 17:6)** *I have called upon Thee, for thou wilt hear me, O God: incline Thine ear unto me, and hear my speech.* As we have read earlier, all prayers are heard by our Lord and all prayers are answered according to God's will. So, with a Christian calling out unto the Lord through prayer and meditation it is our way to communicate with Him. Only by the renewing of our mind and by walking in the spirit can we have direct communication with the Lord. This will be an open line that we can pick up and call anytime upon our heavenly Father during our times of distress. We can lift our voice and His name to give Him holy praise and thanks, to ask for His leadership and guidance.

Walking in a Christ-like manner and having renewed our mind is a daily walk with the Lord. The renewing of our mind is not just a one-time thing, it is a daily event. satan will attack us every day and try to get us out of the line of God and get Him off our minds so that we will not pray. Therefore, God will not lead us and guide us accordingly. This would be satan's will and desire for us, to keep us separated or separate us from the Lord. So once again we must have tunnel vision toward the Lord, toward Jesus on the cross for what He has done for us and being obedient and trusting the holy Spirit to lead us and guide us.

(Romans 12:2) *And be not conformed to this world: but be ye transformed by the renewing of your mind, that ye may prove what is that good, and acceptable, and perfect, will of God.*

(Romans 8:26) *Likewise the Spirit also helpeth our infirmities: for we know not what we should pray for as we ought: but the Spirit Itself maketh intercession for us with groanings which cannot be uttered.*

(Philippians 4:6) *Be careful for nothing; but in every thing by prayer and supplication with thanksgiving let your requests be made known unto God.*

(Hebrews 4:14) *Seeing then that we have a great high priest, that is passed into the heavens, Jesus the Son of God, let us hold fast our profession.*

Giving thanks,

(Ephesians 5:20) *Giving thanks always for all things unto God and the Father in the name of our Lord Jesus Christ;*

(Colossians 3:15-17) *And let the peace of God rule in your hearts, to the which also ye are called in one body; and be ye thankful.

16 Let the word of Christ dwell in you richly in all wisdom; teaching and admonishing one another in psalms and hymns and spiritual songs, singing with grace in your hearts to the Lord. 17 And whatsoever ye do in word or deed, do all in the name of the Lord Jesus, giving thanks to God and the Father by him.*

(1 Thessalonians 5:18) *In everything give thanks; For this is the will of God in Christ Jesus concerning you*

(Hebrews 13:15) *By Him therefore let us offer the sacrifice of praise to God continually, that is, the fruit of our lips giving thanks to His name.* (Psalms 26:7) *That I may publish with the voice of thanksgiving, and tell of all Thy wondrous works.*

(1 Corinthians 15:57) *But thanks be to God, which giveth us the victory through our Lord Jesus Christ.*

(2 Corinthians 2:14) *Now thanks be unto God, which always causeth us to triumph in Christ, and maketh manifest the savour of His knowledge by us in every place.*

(Philippians 4:6) *Be careful for nothing; but in every thing by prayer and supplication with thanksgiving let your requests be made known unto God.*

(Colossians 1:12) *Giving thanks unto the Father, which hath made us to be partakers of the inheritance of the saints in light:*

On my walk I have drawn closer unto the Lord and can feel His Spirit. I'm here in spirit therefore I listen and obey. He helps to lead and guide us. Once again, I'm thankful for the blood of Jesus giving me eternity with God the Father, Jesus the son, and the holy Spirit. I'm so thankful for all things and continually give thanks for everything that the Lord has given to me. Being drawn closer to the Spirit and Him drawing closer to me is such blissfulness.

I have to say that I've just recently encountered during my walk, one short story about thankfulness.

My wife and I was traveling for our honeymoon and needed gas. We stopped by a gas station and the attendant started pumping our gas. I got involved into a conversation with him as we were waiting. The man spoke to me of the different tough times that he was going through at this point in his life. They were concerning his job, losing hours. They were also concerning his rent going up and along with some other tragic events that he was facing.

I on the other hand was telling him how we were getting to travel and see God's beautiful countryside. As the gas finished pumping and we continued our conversation I was inclined to hand this man money from my wallet. As I reached into my wallet and pulled out the money, an unknown amount, just knowing that this is what I should do. I'm guessing $20 or $60, somewhere around there. When I handed this man the money and told him God bless and hope things get better for him, then he was overjoyed, I mean ecstatic.

I could hear the excitement and the gratitude in his voice. As we were pulling away from there, I started talking to my wife about how good that made me feel when that man expressed his gratitude towards me. I truly believe full heartedly that giving that money to him has blessed me by his reactions and thankfulness more than it had blessed him. It enlightens one's soul when we do something kind for another, especially a stranger, and they have so much appreciation for it. It's just like things happen in a chain reaction events that occur. It leads me to want to help others so I can receive this feeling again.

I have felt like this all my life, even when I was not saved or at the point before Jesus had called me unto Himself. My wife and I started talking after we left there about thankfulness. This word has been on my mind for a few months. The Lord has been dealing with me on this topic and hence this is a chapter in the book. What I do know is that we are supposed to give thanks for all things. (Ephesians 5:20).

Something else that I do know is that all things happen for the good of those that love the Lord. (Romans 8:28). As we walk on this earth, rest assured that we will find grateful people and ungrateful people. The more I pray and look for the Lord's guidance and leadership, the more thankful I become. The closer that we walk as Jesus would have us to, then the more thankful we do become, which ultimately draws the Spirit of God closer to every believer. As we become so thankful and overjoyed for things that we are given, knowing that the giver feels the love and expresses it by bestowing other blessings upon us. The more we thank our heavenly Father above for the blessings that we get, He will know that we truly appreciate them, and continue to shower us with blessings.

This includes little blessings and great blessings. The more we do give thanks and appreciate them true heartedly and full heartedly, not just by word but by sincere emotions, then he will draw closer to us. He will feel the thankfulness that we have in our hearts for what He is giving us. Beyond a shadow of a doubt following the Spirit on a daily walk, we will absolutely know that giving thanks unto Him draws His Spirit closer to us.

CHAPTER 7

God's Wrath

In the beginning God was, in the past God has been, in the present God is, and in the future yet to come, God will always be the same. **(Psalms 145:20)** *The LORD preserveth all them that love Him: but all the wicked He will destroy.* **(John 3:36)** *He that believeth on the Son hath everlasting life: and he that believeth not on the Son shall not see life; but the wrath of God abideth on him.*

Listen, there are only two different choices. No more, no less. Only two choices. God or satan.

As we read books of the Old Testament and as the prophets have prophesized and told the stories of the beginning of time, then we see God's wrath or anger toward disobedience.

Some of God's chosen people was cut off from the book of the living after turning their hearts away from God. After seeing miracles that He did for them walking in the wilderness. Moses smote the rock with his staff in the wilderness when they were thirsty. Everyone and their animals drank of the water. (Numbers 20:11).

The Lord made bread fall from heaven when the people hungered. As this occurred the Lord was testing their hearts. His people continually grumbled against Him and had no thanksgiving of the blessings the Lord bestowed upon them. (Exodus 16:4). This brought the wrath of God upon His chosen people because, they rejected the adoration of the Lord. This displeased the Lord and so the disobedient children will not rest in the Lord. **(Hebrews 3:7-11) *Wherefore (as the Holy Ghost saith, Today if ye will hear His voice, 8 Harden not your hearts, as in the provocation, in the day of temptation in the wilderness: 9 When your fathers tempted Me, proved Me, and saw My works forty years. 10 Wherefore I was grieved with that generation, and said, they do always err in their heart; and they have not known my ways. 11 So, I sware in My wrath, They shall not enter My rest.)***

Throughout time God has shown His wrath and displeasure toward those who choose satan. Sodom and Gomorrah were another prime example of God's wrath. God has shown His wrath and disappointment for mankind during Noah's time, during the great flood of the earth. Noah was the only one that was righteous in the Lord's eyes. (Genesis 6:9). Mankind, God's creation, had displeased Him from all their disobedience. (Genesis 6:5-

6). God was sorrowful of his creation. (Genesis 6:7). The sin and wickedness of man was evil. They had absolutely no thanksgiving for what the Lord God had given them and done for them.

Through all of time we have seen disobedience in God's creation and how it has brought His wrath down. We should learn from the past and become better in the present. We have The Holy Bible today; this is God's word that enlightens us to what He would want us to be. This is our heavenly Father speaking directly to us through the old prophets and the apostles and His only begotten son Jesus Christ. (John 1:14).

The Bible has always looked forward to the cross in the Old Testament and to the cross of Calvary when Jesus walked this earth. Today in this time, we look back to the cross of Calvary. We must turn from our wicked sinful nature and walk in the spirit and let God lead our paths. If we don't let God's Spirit lead us, then we are headed for destruction. Hell's fire.

It has been said, earlier in this book, that there are only two sides, two masters, and two ways of life. This is good and evil, light and dark, love and hate. The Lord says if we are not with Him then we are against Him. (Matthew 12:30). I do believe that Psalms 69 is talking from the thoughts of our Lord before and during the crucifixion. One of these verses talks about being cut out of the book of the living. (Psalms 69:28).

This is such a chilling fact to me, knowing the truth, woe to those who don't accept Jesus as their Lord and Savior. As I know that every knee shall bow, and every tongue shall confess my Savior Jesus Christ is Lord. (Romans 14:11). Then His enemies shall be cast into the lake of fire for all eternity with satan and his followers. Anyone that is not in the Lamb's Book of Life, the book of the living, they will be cast into hells fire with the devil and his angels for all eternity. (Revelation 20:15).

There is a judgement and a day to receive our rewards. (2 Corinthians 5:10). I sure do look forward to receiving and being rewarded by my Lord. I sure do feel sad for anyone that has missed the mark and not accepted Jesus as their Lord and Savior. We are only here for a moment on this earth. (James 4:14). I don't know how many times the Lord will call us unto Himself but, if we miss that calling and continue to serve satan then we are on our way towards destruction.

There will be gnashing of teeth and weeping and blazing fire. It will be a place of darkness and separation from the Lord. (Matthew 13:42). There will be a day that every knee will bow, and every tongue will confess that Jesus is Lord. (Philippians 2:10-11). Please heed the reception of these words. This is very serious. There is no second chance. There is no do-overs.

When this day is at hand, the Christians that have accepted Jesus as their Lord and Savior will be overjoyed with their accomplishments and rewards of serving the Lord rightfully. The people that have rejected Jesus as their Lord will be sent to eternal pain and suffering; this will be their worse day that will last the rest of their lives. They will be permanently and eternally separated from our Lord in darkness forever and ever. What a very sad situation this will be. satan will drag many of God's children to hell with him for their disobedience and rejection of the Lord. (Matthew 25:41).

There's a straight and narrow path that the Bible talks about, and how we must follow it to enter the kingdom of Heaven. There is a broad and wide path that takes people to hell and easy is the way for satan is cunning and very deceptive. (Matthew 7:13). The Bible tells us that we know not the hour or day when the Son of man is coming back in the clouds of glory. (Matthew 25:13). What this is saying is that when we die there is no time or day known to man. This means that when we die, the next thing we will face is our Lord Jesus Christ.

Life is short and we must find God. Only the saved will accept Jesus as their Lord and Savior and know that He was crucified for an atonement for our sins. We will be saved by faith through God's grace. Anyone who does not accept these facts and love these facts will be sent to hell. There is no padding over the situation, this is a fact.

There are only two choices to choose from while walking this earth. There is right and there is wrong. There is good and there is evil. There is God and there is mammon. There is heaven and there is hell. It's our choice people on which place we want to spend eternity. We are all given the same opportunity and everything here as we walk on this earth happens to the good and to the bad. (Matthew 5:45).

There is a story that I have heard. Maybe you have also heard this story. There was an old Indian chief and his grandson would come listen to his stories. The grandson had a dream about two wolves fighting, a white wolf and a black wolf. These wolves were fighting every night in his dreams. The grandson come to ask the chief what the meaning of the dream was?

As the chief listened to what his grandson had dreamed about, he told his grandson that we walk through a spiritual warfare every day in life. The black wolf is the devil and his demons. The white wolf is the Lord and His angels. There is a battle in our minds every day, a spiritual warfare. As the chief continued to explain this to his grandson then a question arose from the grandson. What wolf will win the fight in the end? The chief answered saying, the wolf you feed. This is common sense. If we feed one of these wolves, then it will become stronger and overcome the other one.

God is almighty, powerful, and stronger than satan but, if we feed satan then he will have victory over us because, we are weak without the Lord. If we feed off the Lord, then He will strengthen us and give us the power to defeat satan. My strength is in the Lord and comes from the Lord. (Psalms 18:1-3). Who will you choose in your walk here on the earth? satan will lead you to hell.

God will lead you to the place that He has prepared for His children with Him for all eternity. Once we receive and accept the holy Spirit that will dwell within all believers, then we can feel His comfort, peace, love, and joy within us on our daily walk. If we deny God's Spirit to dwell within us, then satan will reign our lives and we will be full of misery, hate, lies, and deceit. satan is a liar. (John 8:44). He will deceive you and only looks for whom he can devour and destroy. (1 Peter 5:8). It's so plain to see that there are only two choices in this life, God or satan. There is no middle choice, no grey area, no room for lukewarm. You are either hot or cold for the Lord. (Revelation 3:15-16).

God will show mercy to those that accept Jesus as their Lord and Savior. God will show wrath toward those that deny His only begotten Son. Isaiah prophesied back in the Old Testament of Jesus at Calvary. He talks about one that is beaten and smitten for our sins and afflicted for our iniquities. (Isaiah 53:5).

Psalms 69 references Jesus thoughts, feelings, emotions, and prayers during the time of Calvary.

Jesus was given to us by God, His only begotten son, that we may have life and have it more abundantly. (John 10:10). Don't be deceived by satan. If we deny this gift and don't accept God's grace, then there will be hell to pay. We can't pad this over or push it away, it is a fact in God's word. The sinner will spend eternity in hell with satan and his angels.

There will be wrath at the end days and I sure would hate to be on that end of a bad decision. I am thankful to the Lord. I am thankful that His wrath will not fall upon me. It is a blessing to know what I know, and to feel what I feel. I have been out of the way and headed in the direction that the Lord would not have me to trod and then I felt the chastening of His hand. This is the love of the heavenly Father that was correcting my wrongdoing.

There is a difference between chastening and wrath. Chastening is for a temporary time that brings children back into the line that they should be walking. Wrath is for all eternity and there is no turning back from that. There are stories of God's wrath throughout the Bible. We can study it in the Old Testament and see the wrath He had toward His specific people, His chosen people, the Israelites.

God is just and fair. It doesn't matter about His chosen people, if their disobedient and don't receive Jesus and accept the drawing (calling) of the Spirit, they will receive His wrath as He has said. As we have seen and read God will bring His wrath down upon His chosen people, then we must surely know that He will bring His wrath down upon the different nations aside from Israel. The New Testament talks about God's wrath in the days of Noah and about God's wrath in Sodom and Gomorrah.

(2 Peter 2:5-6). The book of Revelations speaks of God's wrath to come in the end days. God's wrath will come.

People can pad it over or say Jesus is love and things are different now than they were in the Old Testament. Well, Jesus is love, God is love. (1 John 4:16). This fact doesn't mean that we can be disobedient or turn down the grace given to us by God through His only begotten son. God is the same; in the beginning, in the present, and in the future, Never changing. Overall, there is only one way to escape the wrath of God.

When the holy Spirit calls us unto Himself, then we must answer. We must accept Jesus as our Lord and Savior. Don't deny Him, He has done everything for us. He is our only escape from the wrath of God. (1Thessalonians 1:10). The Lord does not want us to spend eternity in hell with satan and his demons.

However, if we do not accept Jesus, then that is where we belong. Once again, there are only two sides in life. God doesn't want to bring His wrath upon us because hell was created for the devil and his angels. He would rather we accept Jesus Christ as our Lord and Savior and not perish into hell's eternal flame. (1 Thessalonians 5:9).

We pray that those of you who read this book make the right decision while you are still breathing here in this world. After this world is over and your life ends here on earth, if you haven't made the right decision, there will be dues to pay for all eternity. People will be hiding from the wrath of God and there will be no place to hide. (Revelation 6:16-17). We pray that you seek the Lord, and that you will rejoice with us in heaven after Jesus has come to gather His church. In Jesus name we pray, Amen.

CONCLUSION

<u>Plan of Salvation:</u>

God has given us a simple plan to follow that we may spend eternity with Him in heaven. By reading these simple instructions, it appears that this would be an easy walk, but satan has other plans for us. To correctly follow the Lord in this flesh and blood, during this walk here on earth, it will be the hardest thing that we must accomplish here. Only by Gods Spirit are we able to overcome the sinful nature that is within us. This is an absolute lifestyle change but, if we don't commit our lives unto the Lord, we will spend eternity in hell with the devil and his angels. Take heed of Gods word and be ye transformed.

A. Romans 3:23-For all have sinned, and come short of the glory of God;

- Since the beginning of man, starting with Adam we have come short of Gods expectations. Adam sinned in the Garden of Eden and this brought a sinful nature upon all men at their birth. We cannot escape this fact; we are born into sin.

B. Romans 6:23-For the wages of sin is death; but the gift of God is eternal life through Jesus Christ our Lord.

- God is pure, and satan is sin. God despises sin but has given us a path to get through it. Only by the blood of His son Jesus Christ are we saved. The salvation is not by works or anything that we can do but is a gift from the Almighty God. This gift and by the blood of Jesus we shall inherit the kingdom of heaven.

C. Romans 5:8-But God commendeth His love toward us, in that, while we were yet sinners, Christ died for us.
- Jesus was smitten of God and afflicted for our infirmities. Even though He was a man that walked this earth and was found sinless before the Lord, He took on the sins of the whole world. Jesus did not know the feeling of guilt or sin until He hung on the cross at Calvary. This is true love that God has given unto all that accept Him.

D. 2 Timothy 1:9-Who hath saved us, and called us with an holy calling, not according to our works, but according His own purpose and grace, which was given us in Christ Jesus before the world began,
- During our walk here on earth God calls to each and everyone of us in our lives. This is everyone being drawn by the holy Spirit of God.

Once again, there are only two ways, two different decisions, two choices that we can make in this world. We can say yes and accept the graciousness of our Lords Spirit calling unto us. The Bible tells us that many are called but few are chosen. We can say no and deny this precious gift that will last until all eternity. The Bible tells us few are chosen because few accept Jesus as their Lord and Savior. Everyone, on this earth has the same opportunity to live in peace and happiness for all eternity with Jesus in heaven. On the other hand, those that don't accept him, will live with pain and misery in hells fire with the devil and his angels.

E. Acts 2:38-Then Peter said unto them, Repent, and be baptized everyone of you in Jesus Christ for the remission of your sins, and ye shall receive the gift of the Holy Ghost.
- Upon being called, being drawn, being led to give our lives to God, if we give an affirmative answer and accept this calling then we shall be saved. When we do accept Jesus Christ as our Lord and Savior then we are baptized by fire. Being baptized by

fire means receiving the Holy Ghost unto our person. From this point forward the holy Spirit will dwell within every believer. The holy Spirit was given unto us that we may be led, understand, and have the laws of God written upon our hearts. His Spirit will lead us and guide us into all truth, showing us the path we must trod. Once we are sealed by the holy Spirit during this baptism of fire then we shall be saved and wait upon our Lord Jesus to come redeem us in the final days.

Conclusion of conclusion:

God will call unto all of us. We can accept and live for Him, which will bring us to heaven. If we deny His calling, then we are choosing satan. After we choose satan then we will live in hells fire for all eternity. The choice is yours as it is everyone's. Once we die in the flesh then there is no second chance, no do overs, no other way but the decision that we have made. Please think hard, meditate, and pray fervently for the understanding of God's word and the drawing of His Spirit that ye shall be saved.

Scripture Index

1 Corinthians 3:2 I have fed you with milk, and not with meat: for hitherto ye were not able to bear it, neither yet now are ye able.

1 Corinthians 3:16 Know ye not that ye are the temple of God, and that the Spirit of God dwelleth in you?

1 Corinthians 11:31 For if we would judge ourselves, we should not be judged.

1 Corinthians 12:12 For as the body is one, and hath many members, and all the members of that one body, being many, are one body: so also is Christ.

1 Corinthians 15:57 But thanks be to God, which giveth us the victory through our Lord Jesus Christ.

2 Corinthians 2:14 Now thanks be unto God, which always causeth us to triumph in Christ, and maketh manifest the savour of His knowledge by us in every place.

2 Corinthians 5:10 For we must all appear before the judgement seat of Christ; that every one may receive the things done in his body, according to that he hath done, whether it be good or bad.

2 Corinthians 5:17 Therefore if any man be in Christ, he is a new creature: old things are passed away; behold, all things are become new.

2 Corinthians 12:9 And he said unto me, My grace is sufficient for thee: for my strength is made perfect in weakness. Most gladly therefore will I rather glory in my infirmities, that the power of Christ may rest upon me.

1 John 1:8 If we say that we have no sin, we deceive ourselves, and the truth is not in us.

1 John 2:1 My little children, these things write I unto you, that ye sin not. And if any man sin, we have an advocate with the Father, Jesus Christ the righteous:

1 John 2:2 And He is propitiation for our sins: and not for ours only, but also for the sins of the whole world.

1 John 2:17 And the world passeth away, and the lusts thereof: but he that doeth the will of God abideth for ever.

1 John 4:1 Beloved, believe not every spirit, but try the spirits whether they are of God: because many false prophets are gone out into the world.

1 John 4:7-8 Beloved, let us love one another: for love is of God; and every one that loveth is born of God, and knoweth God. 8 He that loveth not, knoweth not God; for God is love.

1 John 4:16 And we have known and believed the love that God hath to us. God is love; and he that dwelleth in love dwelleth in God, and God in him.

1 John 4:19 We love Him, because He first loved us.

1 John 5:14-15 And this is the confidence that we have in Him, that if we ask any thing according to His will He heareth us. 15 And if we know that He hear us, whatsoever we ask, we know that we have the petitions that we desired of Him.

1Peter 3:15 But sanctify the Lord God in your hearts: and be ready always to give an answer to every man that asketh you a reason of the hope that is in you with meekness and fear:

1 Peter 5:8 Be sober, be vigilant; because your adversary the devil, as a roaring lion, walketh about, seeking whom he may devour:

2 Peter 2:2-3 And many shall follow their pernicious ways; by reason of whom the way of truth shall be evil spoken of. 3 And through covetousness shall they with feigned words make merchandise of you: whose judgement now of a long time lingereth not, and their damnation slumbereth not.

2 Peter 2:5-6 And spared not the old world, but saved Noah the person, a preacher of righteousness, bringing in the flood upon the world of the ungodly; 6 And turning the cities of Sodom and Gomorrha into ashes condemned them with an overthrow, making them an ensample unto those that after should live ungodly; 2 Peter 2:22 But it is happened unto them according to the true proverb, The dog is turned to his own vomit again; and the sow that was washed to her wallowing in the mire.

1 Thessalonians 1:10 And to wait for His Son from heaven, whom He was raised from the dead, even Jesus, which delivered us from the wrath to come.

1 Thessalonians 5:9 For God hath not appointed us to wrath, but to obtain salvation by our Lord Jesus Christ,

1 Thessalonians 5:17-19 Pray without ceasing. 18 In ever thing give thanks; for this is the will of God in Christ Jesus concerning you. 19 Quench not the Spirit.

1 Timothy 2:5 For there is one God, and one mediator between God and men, the man Christ Jesus;

2 Timothy 1:7 For God hath not given us the spirit of fear; but of power, and of love, and of a sound mind.

2 Timothy 2:15 Study to show thyself approved unto God, a workman that needeth not to be ashamed, rightly dividing the word of truth.

Acts 3:19 Repent ye therefore, and be converted, that your sins may be blotted out, when the times of refreshing shall come from the presence of the Lord;

Acts 16:31 And they said, Believe on the Lord Jesus Christ, and now shall be saved, and thy house.

Colossians 1:12 Giving thanks unto the Father, which hath made us meet to be partakers of the inheritance of the saints in light:

Colossians 1:14 In whom we have redemption through His blood, even the forgiveness of sins:

Colossians 1:18 And He is the head of the body, the church: who is the beginning, the first born from the dead; that in all things He might have the preeminence.

Colossians 2:12-13 Buried with Him in baptism, wherein also ye are risen with Him through the faith of the operation of God, who hath raised Him from the dead. 13 And you, being dead in your sins and the uncircumcision of your flesh, hath He quickened together with Him, having forgiven you all trespasses;

Colossians 3:15-17 And let the peace of God rule in your hearts, to the which also ye are called in one body; and be ye thankful. 16 Let the word of Christ dwell in you richly in all wisdom; teaching and admonishing one another in psalms and hymns and spriritual songs, singing with grace in your hearts to the Lord. 17 And whatsoever ye do in word or deed, do all in the name of the Lord Jesus, giving thanks to God and the Father by him.

Colossians 3:23 And whatsoever ye do, do it heartily, as to the Lord, and not unto men;

Deuteronomy 8:5-6 Thou shall also consider in thine heart, that, as a man chasteneth his son, so the Lord thy God chasteneth thee. 6 Therefore thou shalt keep the commandments of the Lord thy God, to walk in His ways, and to fear Him.

Ecclesiastes 12:7 Then shall the dust return to the earth as it was: and the spirit shall return unto God who gave it.

Ephesians 1:4-5 According as He hath chosen us in Him before the foundation of the world, that we should be holy and without blame before Him in love: 5

Having predestinated us unto the adoption of children by Jesus Christ to Himself, according to the good pleasure of His will,

Ephesians 1:13-14 In whom ye also trusted, after that ye heard the word of truth, the gospel of your salvation: in whom also after that ye believed, ye were sealed with that holy Spirit of promise, 14 Which is the earnest of our inheritance until the redemption of the purchased possession, unto the praise of His glory.

Ephesians 2:8 For by grace are ye saved through faith; and that not of yourselves: it is the gift of God:

Ephesians 5:4 Neither filthiness, nor foolish talking, nor jesting, which are not convenient: but rather giving thanks.

Ephesians 5:20 Giving thanks always for all things unto God and the Father in the name of our Lord Jesus Christ;

Ephesians 5:26 That He might sanctify and cleanse it with the washing of water by the word,

Ephesians 6:4 And, ye fathers, provoke not your children to wrath: but bring them up in the nurture and admonition of the Lord.

Ephesians 6:10 Finally, my brethren, be strong in the Lord, and in the power of His might.

Ephesians 6:11-12 Put on the whole armor of God, that ye may be able to stand against the whiles of the devil. 12 For we wrestle not against flesh and blood, but against principalities, against powers, against the rulers of darkness of this world, against spiritual wickedness in high places.

Ephesians 6:16 Above all, taking the shield of faith, wherewith ye shall be able to quench all the fiery darts of the wicked.

Ephesians 6:18-20 Praying always with all prayer and supplication in the Spirit, and watching thereunto with all perseverance and supplication for all saints; 19

And for me, that utterance may be given unto me, that I may open my mouth boldly, to make known the mystery of the gospel, 20 For which I am an ambassador in bonds: that therein I may speak boldly, as I ought to speak.

Exodus 16:4 Then said the Lord to Moses, Behold, I will rain bread from heaven for you; and the people shall go out and gather a certain rate every day, that I may prove them, whether they will walk in My law, or no.

Galatians 1:15 But when it pleased God, who separated me from my mother's womb, and called me by His grace,

Galatians 3:26-27 For ye are all the children of God by faith in Christ Jesus. 27 For as many of you have been baptized into Christ have put on Christ.

Genesis 6:5-6 And God saw that the wickedness of man was great in the earth, and that every imagination of the thoughts of his heart was only evil continually. 6 And it repented the Lord that He had made man on the earth, and it grieved Him at His heart.

Genesis 6:7 And the Lord said, I will destroy man whom I have created from the face of the earth; both man, and beast, and the creeping thing; and the fowls of the air; for it repenteth Me that I have made them.

Genesis 6:9 These are the generations of Noah: Noah was a just man and perfect in his generations, and Noah walked with God.

Hebrews 3:7-11 Wherefore (as the Holy Ghost saith, Today, if ye will hear His voice, 8 Harden not your hearts, as in the provocation, in the day of temptation in the wilderness: 9 When your fathers tempted Me, proved Me, and saw My works forty years. 10

Wherefore I was grieved with that generation, and said, They do alway err in their heart; and they have not known My ways. 11 So I sware in My wrath, They shall not enter into My rest.)

Hebrews 4:13 Neither is there any creature that is not manifest in His sight: but all things are naked and opened unto the eyes of Him with whom we have to do.

Hebrews 4:14 Seeing then that we have a great high priest, that is passed into the heavens, Jesus the Son of God, let us hold fast our profession.

Hebrews 11:6 But without faith it is possible to please Him: for he that cometh to God must believe that He is, and that He is a rewarder of them that diligently seek him.

Hebrews 12:5-11 And ye have forgotten the exhortation which speaketh unto you as unto children, My son, despise not thou the chastening of the Lord, nor faint when thou art rebuked of Him: 6 For whom the Lord loveth He chasteneth, and scourgeth every son whom He receiveth. 7 If ye endure chastening, God dealeth with you as with sons; for what son is he whom the father chasteneth not? 8 But if ye be without chastisement, wereof all are partakers, then are ye bastards, and not sons. 9 Furthermore we have had fathers of our flesh which corrected us, and we gave them reverence: shall we not much rather be in subjection unto the Father of spirits, and live? 10

For they verily for a few days chastened us after their own pleasure; but He for our profit, that we might be partakers of His holiness. 11 Now no chastening for the present seemeth to be joyous, but grievous: nevertheless afterward it yieldeth the peaceable fruit of righteousness unto them which are exercised thereby.

Hebrews 13:5-6 Let your conversation be without covetousness; and be content with such things as ye have: for He hath said, I will never leave thee, nor forsake thee. 6 So that we may boldly say, The Lord is my helper, and I will not fear what man shall do unto me.

Hebrew 13:8 Jesus Christ the same yesterday, and to day, and for ever.

Hebrews 13:15 By Him therefore let us offer the sacrifice of praise to God continually, that is, the fruits of our lips giving thanks to His name.

Isaiah 53:5 But He was wounded for our transgressions, He was bruised for our iniquities; the chastisement of our peace was upon Him; and with His stripes we are healed.

James 1:19 Wherefore, my beloved brethren, let every man be swift to hear, slow to speak, slow to wrath:

James 4:3 Ye ask, and receive not, because ye ask amiss, that ye may consume it upon your lusts.

James 4:10 Humble yourselves in the sight of the Lord, and He shall lift you up.

James 4:14 Whereas ye know not what shall be on morrow. For what is your life? It is even a vapor, that appeareth for a little time, and then vanisheth away.

James 5:16 Confess your faults one to another, and pray one for another, that ye may be healed. The effectual fervent prayer of a righteous man availeth much.

James 5:20 Let him know, that which converteth the sinner from error of his way shall save a soul from death, and shall hide a multitude of sins.

Jeremiah 3:22 Return, ye backsliding children, and I will heal your backslidings. Behold, we come unto Thee; for Thou art the Lord our God.

Jeremiah 29:11 For I know the thoughts that I think toward you, saith the Lord, thoughts of peace, and not of evil, to give you an expected end.

Job 5:17 Behold, happy is the man whom God correcteth: therefore despise not thou the chastening of the Almighty:

John 1:14 And the Word was made flesh, and dwelt among us, (and we beheld His glory, the glory as of the only begotten of the Father,) full of grace and truth.

John 1:27 He it is, who coming after me is preferred before me, whose shoe's latchet I am not worthy to unloose.

John 3:16 For God so loved the world, that He gave His only begotten Son, that whosoever believeth in Him should not perish, but have everlasting life.

John 3:36 He that believeth on the Son hath everlasting life: and he that believeth not the Son shall not see life; but the wrath of God abideth on him.

John 5:30 I can of Mine own self do nothing: as I hear, I judge: and My judgement is just; because I seek not Mine own will, but the will of the Father which hath sent Me.

John 5:39 Search the scriptures; for in them ye think ye have eternal life: and they are they which testify of Me.

John 8:36 If the Son therefore shall make you free, ye shall be free indeed.

John 8:44 Ye are your father the devil, and the lusts of the father ye will do. He was a murderer from the beginning, and abode not in the truth, because there is no truth in him. When he speaketh a lie, he speaketh of his own: for he is a liar, and the father of it.

John 10:10 The thief cometh not, but for to steal, and to kill, and to destroy: I am come that they might have life, and they might have it more abundantly.

John 13:34 A new commandment I give unto you, That ye love one another; as I have loved you, that ye also love one another.

John 14:2-4 In My Father's house are many mansions: if it were not so, I would have told you. I go to prepare a place for you. 3 And if I go and prepare a place for you, I will come again, and receive you unto

Myself; that where I am, there ye may be also. 4 And whither I go ye know, and the way ye know.

John 14:16-21 And I will pray the Father, and He shall give you another Comforter, that He may abide with you for ever; 17 Even the Spirit of truth; whom the world cannot receive, because it seeth Him not, neither knoweth Him: but ye know Him; for He dwelleth with you, and shall be in you. 18 I will not leave you comfortless: I will come to you. 19 Yet a little while, and the world seeth Me no more; but ye see Me: because I live, ye shall live also. 20 At that day ye shall know that I am in My Father, and ye in Me, and I in you. 21 He that hath My commandments, and keepeth them, he it is that loveth Me: and he that loveth Me shall be loved of My Father, and I will love him, and will manifest Myself to him.

John 15:4-5 Abide in Me, and I in you. As the branch cannot bear fruit of itself, except it abide in the vine; no more can ye, except ye abide in Me. 5 I am the vine, ye are the branches: He that abideth in Me, and I in him, the same bringeth forth much fruit: for without

Me ye can do nothing.

John 15:13 Greater love hath no man than this, that a man lay down his life for his friends.

John 16:8 And when He is come, He will reprove the world of sin, and of righteousness, and of judgement:

John 16:13 Howbeit when He, the Spirit of truth, is come, He will guide you into all truth: for He shall not speak of Himself; but whatsoever He shall hear, that shall He speak: and He will shew your things to come.

John 16:33 These things I have spoken unto you, that in Me ye might have peace. In the world ye shall have tribulation: but be of good cheer; I have overcome the world.

Jonah 2:2 And said, I cried by reason of mine affliction unto the Lord, and He heard me; out of the belly of hell cried I, and Thou heardest my voice.

Luke 3:16 John answered, saying unto to them all, I indeed baptize you with water; but one mightier than I cometh, the latchet of whose shoes I am not worthy to unloose: He shall baptize you with the Holy Ghost and fire:

Luke 6:31 And as ye would that men should do to you, do ye also to them likewise.

Luke 9:62 And Jesus said unto him, No man, having put his hand to the plow, and looking back, is fit for the kingdom of God.

Luke 12:12 For the Holy Ghost shall teach you in the same hour what ye ought to say.

Mark 11:24 Therefore I say unto you, What things soever ye desire, when we pray, believe that ye receive them, and ye shall have them.

Mark 12:30-31 And thou shalt love the Lord thy God with all thy heart, and with all thy soul, and with all thy mind, and with all thy strength: this is the first commandment. 31 And the second is like, namely this,

Thou shalt love thy neighbor as thyself. There is none other commandment greater than these.

Matthew 5:15 Neither do men light a candle, and put it under a bushel, but on a candlestick; and it giveth light unto all that are in the house.

Matthew 5:16 Let your light so shine before men, that they may see your good works, and glorify your Father which is in heaven.

Matthew 5:37 But let your communication be, Yea, yea; Nay, nay: for whatsoever is more than these cometh of evil.

Matthew 5:44 But I say unto you, Love your enemies, bless them that curse you, do good to them that hate you, and pray for them which despitefully use you, and persecute you;

Matthew 5:45 That ye may be children of your Father which is in heaven: for He maketh His sun to rise on the evil and on the good, and sendeth rain on the just and on the unjust.

Mathew 6:6 But thou, when thou prayest, enter into thy closet, and when thou hast shut thy door, pray to thy Father which is in secret; and thy Father which seeeth in secret shall reward thee openly.

Matthew 6:9-13 After this manner therefore pray ye: Our Father which art in heaven, Hallowed be Thy name. 10 Thy kingdom come, Thy will be done in earth, as it is in heaven. 11 Give us this day our daily bread. 12 And forgive us our debts, as we forgive our debtors. 13 And lead us not into temptation, but deliver us from evil: For Thine is the kingdom, and the power, and the glory, for ever. Amen.

Matthew 6:19-21 Lay not up for yourselves treasures upon earth, where moth and rust doth corrupt, and where thieves break through and steal: 20 But lay up for yourselves treasures in heaven, where neither moth nor rust doth corrupt, and where thieves do not break through nor steal: 21 For where your treasure is, there will your heart be also.

Matthew 6:24 No man can serve two masters: for either he will hate the one, and love the other; or else he will hold to the one, and despise the other. Ye cannot serve God and mammon.

Matthew 6:33 But seek ye first the kingdom of God, and His righteousness; and all these things shall be added unto you.

Matthew 7:1 JUDGE not, that ye be not judged.

Matthew 7:3 And why beholdest thou the mote that is in thy brother's eye, but considerest not the beam that is thy own eye?

Matthew 7:7 Ask, and it shall be given; seek, and ye shall find; knock, and it shall be opened unto you:

Matthew 7:12 Therefore all things whatsoever ye would that men should do to you, do ye even so to them: for this is the law and the prophets.

Matthew 7:13-14 Enter ye in at the strait gate: for wide is the gate, and broad is the way, that leadeth to destruction, and many there be which go in thereat:

14 Because strait is the gate, and narrow is the way, which leadeth unto life, and few there be that find it.

Matthew 7:16-20 Ye shall know them by their fruits.

Do men gather grapes of thorns, or figs of thistles? 17

Even so every good tree bringeth forth good fruit; but a corrupt tree bringeth forth evil fruit. 18 A good tree cannot bring forth evil fruit, neither can a corrupt tree bring forth good fruit. 19 Every tree that bringeth not forth good fruit is hewn down, and cast into the fire.

20 Wherefore by their fruits ye shall know them.

Matthew 11:30 For My yoke is easy, and My burden is light.

Matthew 12:30 He that is not with Me is against Me; and he that gathereth not with Me scattereth abroad.

Matthew 12:43-45 When the unclean spirit is gone out of a man, he walketh through dry places, seeking rest, and findeth none. 44 Then he saith, I will return into my house from whence I came out; and when he is come, he findeth it empty, swept, and garnished. 45

Then goeth he, and taketh with himself seven other spirits more wicked than himself, and they enter in and dwell there: and the last state of that man is worse than the first. Even so shall it be also unto this wicked generation.

Matthew 13:42 And shall cast them into a furnace of fire: there shall be wailing and gnashing of teeth.

Matthew 16:24 Then said Jesus unto his disciples, If any man will come after Me, let him deny himself, and take up his cross, and follow Me.

Matthew 17:16-20 And I brought him to Thy disciples, and they could not cure him. 17 Then Jesus answered and said, O faithless and perverse generation, how long shall I be with you? How long shall I suffer you? bring him hither to Me. 18 And Jesus rebuked the devil; and he departed out of him; and the child was cured from that very hour. 19 Then came the disciples to Jesus apart, and said, Why could not we cast him out? 20 And Jesus said unto them, Because of your unbelief; for verily I say unto you, If ye have faith as a grain of mustard seed, ye shall say unto this mountain, Remove hence to yonder place; and it shall remove; and nothing shall be impossible unto you.

Matthew 22:39 And the second is unto it, Thou shalt love thy neighbor as thyself.

Matthew 25:13 Watch therefore, for ye know neither the day nor the hour wherein the Son of Man cometh.

Matthew 25:41 Then shall he say unto them on the left hand, Depart from me ye cursed, into everlasting fire, prepared for the devil and his angels:

Matthew 5:38-42 Ye have heard that it hath been said, An eye for and eye, and a tooth for a tooth: 39

But I say unto you, That ye resist not evil: but whosoever shall smite thee on the right cheek, turn to him the other also. 40 And if any man will sue thee at the law, and take away thy coat, let him have thy cloak also. 41 And whosoever shall compel thee to go a mile, go with him twain. 42 Give to him that asketh thee, and from him that would borrow of thee turn not thou away.

Numbers 20:11 And Moses lifted up his hand, and with his rod he smote the rock twice: and the water came out abundantly, and the congregation drank, and their beasts also.

Philippians 1:6 Being confident of this very thing, that He which hath begun a good work in you will perform it until the day of Jesus Christ:

Philippians 2:10-11 That at the name of Jesus every knee should bow, of things in heaven, and things in earth, and things under the earth; 11 And that every tongue should confess that Jesus Christ is Lord, to the glory of God the Father.

Philippians 4:6 Be careful for nothing; but in every thing by prayer and supplication with thanksgiving let your requests be made known unto God.

Philippians 4:8 Finally, brethren, whatsoever things are true, whatsoever things are honest, whatsoever things are just, whatsoever things are pure, whatsoever things are lovely, whatsoever things are good report; if there be any virtue, and if there be any praise, think on these things.

Philippians 4:9 Those things, which ye have both learned, and received, and heard, and seen in me, do: and the God of peace shall be with you.

Philippians 4:13 I can do all things through Christ which strengtheneth me.

Proverbs 3:11 My son, despise not the chastening of the Lord; neither be weary of His correction:

Proverbs 14:14 The backslider in heart shall be filled with his on ways: and a good man shall be satisfied from himself.

Psalms 18:1-3 I will love Thee, O LORD, my strength.

2 The LORD is my rock, and my fortress, and my deliverer; my God, my strength, in whom I will trust; my buckler, and the horn of my salvation, and my high tower. 3 I will call upon the LORD, who is worthy to be praised: so shall I be saved from mine enemies.

Proverbs 24:9-10 The thought of foolishness is sin: and the scorner is an abomination to men. 10 If thou faint in the day of adversity, thy strength is small.

Proverbs 25:22 For thou shalt heap coals of fire upon his head, and the Lord shall reward thee.

Proverbs 26:11 As a dog returneth to its vomit, so a fool returneth to his folly.

Psalms 1:1 Blessed is the man that walketh not in the counsel of the ungodly, nor standeth in the way of sinners, nor sitteth in the seat of the scornful.

Psalms 4:4 Stand in awe, and sin not: commune with your own heart upon your bed, and be still. Selah.

Psalms 17:6 I have called upon Thee, for thou wilt hear me, O God: incline Thine ear unto me, and hear my speech.

Psalms 18 1-3 I will love Thee, O Lord, my strength. 2

The Lord is my rock, and my fortress, and my deliverer; my God, my strength, in whom I will trust; my buckler, and the horn of my salvation, and my high tower. 3 I will call upon the LORD, who is worthy to be praised: so shall I be saved from mine enemies.

Psalms 26:7 That I may publish with the voice of thanksgiving, and tell of all Thy wondrous works.

Psalms 26:11 But as for me, I will walk in mine integrity: redeem me, and be merciful unto me.

Psalms 27:14 Wait on the Lord: be of good courage, and He shall strengthen thine heart: wait, I say, on the Lord.

Psalms 37:4 Delight thyself also in the Lord; and He shall give thee the desires of the heart.

Psalms 40:1-2 I waited patiently for the Lord; and He inclined unto me, and heard my cry. 2 He brought me up also out of an horrible pit, out of the miry clay, and set my feet upon a rock, and established my goings.

Psalms 50:15 And call upon Me in the day of trouble: I will deliver thee, and now shalt glorify Me.

Psalms 51:12 Restore unto me the joy of Thy salvation; and uphold me with Thy free spirit.

Psalms 66:19 Blessed be God, which hath not turned away my prayer, nor His mercy from me.

Psalms 69:28 Let them be blotted out of the book of the living, and not be written with the righteous.

Psalms 92:1 It is a good thing to give thanks unto the

Lord, and to sing unto Thy name, O Most High:

Psalms 103:12 As far as the east is from the west, so far hath He removed our transgressions from us.

Psalms 139:1-2 O LORD, Thou hast searched me, and known me. 2 Thou knowest my downsitting and mine uprising, Thou understandest my thought afar off.

Psalms 143:10 Teach me to do Thy will; for Thou art my God: Thy Spirit is good; lead me into the land of uprightness.

Psalms 145:20 The LORD preserveth all them that love Him: but all the wicked will He destroy.

Revelation 3:15 I know thy works, that thou are neither cold nor hot: I would thou wert cold or hot.

Revelation 3:16 So then because thou art lukewarm, and neither cold nor hot, I will spew thee out of My mouth.

Revelation 6:16-17 And said to the mountains and rocks, Fall on us, and hide us from the dace of Him that sitteth on the throne, and from the wrath of the Lamb: 17 For the great day of His wrath is come; and who shall be able to stand?

Revelation 20:15 And whosoever was not found written in the book of life was cast into the lake of fire.

Romans 2:1-2 Therefore thou art inexcusable, O man, whosoever thou art that judgest: for wherein thou judgest another, thou condemnest thyself; for thou that judgest doest the same things. 2 But we are sure that the judgement of God is according to truth against them which commit such things.

Romans 2:11 For there is no respect of persons with God.

Romans 3:25 Whom God hath set forth to be a propitiation through faith in His blood, to declare His righteousness for the remission of sins that are past, through the forebearance of God;

Romans 5:3 And not only so, but we glory in tribulations also: knowing that tribulations worketh patience;

Romans 5:8 But God commendeth His love toward us, in that, while we were yet sinners, Christ died for us.

Romans 5:19 For as by one man's disobedience many were made sinners, so by the obedience of One shall many be made righteous.

Romans 6:4 Therefore we are buried with Him by baptism into death: that like as Christ was raised up from the dead by the glory of the Father, even so we should walk in newness of life.

Romans 6:6 Knowing this, that our old man is crucified with Him, that the body of sin might be destroyed, that henceforth we should not serve sin.

Romans 8:11 But if the Spirit of Him that raised up Jesus from the dead dwell in you, He that raised up Christ from the dead shall also quicken your mortal bodies by His Spirit that dwelleth in you.

Romans 8:12 Therefore, brethren, we are debtors, not to the flesh, to live after the flesh.

Romans 8:26 Likewise the Spirit also helpeth our infirmities: for we know not what we should pray for as we ought: but the Spirit Itself maketh intercession for us with groanings which cannot be uttered.

Romans 8:27 And He that searcheth the hearts knoweth what is the mind of the Spirit, because He maketh intercession for the saints according to the will of God.

Romans 8:28 And we know that all things work together for good to them that love God, to them who are the called according to His purpose.

Romans 8:34 Who is he that condemneth? It is Christ that died, yea rather, that is isen again, who is even at the right hand of God, who also maketh intercession for us.

Romans 10:9 That if thou shalt confess with thy mouth the Lord Jesus, and shalt believe in thine heart that God hath raised Him from the dead, thou shalt be saved.

Romans 12:1-2 I BESEECH you therefore, brethren, by the mercies of God, that ye present your bodies a living sacrifice, holy, acceptable unto God, which is your reasonable service. 2 And be not conformed to this world: but be ye transformed by the renewing of your mind, that ye may prove what is good, and acceptable, and perfect, will of God.

Romans 12:6 Having then gifts differing according to the grace that is given to us, whether prophecy, let us prophesy according to the proportion of faith;

Romans 12:12 Rejoicing in hope; patient in tribulation; continuing instant in prayer;

Romans 12:19 Dearly beloved, avenge not yourselves, but rather give place unto wrath: for it is written, Vengeance is Mine; I will repay, saith the Lord.

Romans 14:11 For it is written, As I live, saith the Lord, every knee shall bow to Me, and every tongue shall confess to God.

Romans 15:13 Now he God of hope fill you with all joy and peace in believing, that ye may abound in hope, through the power of the Holy Ghost.

NOTES:

NOTES:

Notes:

CPSIA information can be obtained
at www.ICGtesting.com
Printed in the USA
BVHW071546290719
554566BV00007B/955/P